a boy after the sea

AN UNTOLD STORY

Kevin Snook

Foreword by
Heston Blumenthal

introduction

I was truly overwhelmed by the success of 'a Boy After the Sea', not only because of the chefs who so kindly agreed to be a part of the book, but also the fact it was awarded the 'Best Fish and Seafood' cookery book in the world by the renowned Gourmand Cookbook Awards committee in 2010.

The book in its sombre way allowed me the opportunity to share Dan, my late son's, love of cooking and fishing. Since then I was approached by several acclaimed chefs who expressed an interest in being part of a future publication. A Boy after the Sea 2 was therefore born!

Perhaps in a better state of mind, I was able to see more clearly and could understand that Dan was now living in a happier 'place', and that perhaps he had not taken his own life, but that a tragic accident had simply and sadly taken place.

My new book is therefore a tribute to Dan and his love for nature, and a salute to my other two boys, Christopher and Elliot. It also focuses on the terrible devastation taking place in the world today, through the destruction and plight of our oceans. To this end, I asked the kind assistance of my brother Raymond who in his capacity as a Naval Officer has spent much time researching this very subject. He lovingly agreed to share his knowledge and explain the problems we face and to highlight possible solutions.

I feel honoured and humbled to be in the company of 29 of the most creative chefs in the world today. I have selected these incredible individuals for their conviction, innovation and vision, and their commitment and passion for using sustainable fish resources. They are to be applauded for the notable impact that they are making within their respective countries. My remit was simply for them to present dishes from our oceans using sustainable supplies. This they have magically achieved through their own creative licence!

Equally, I have been sincerely blessed to have the encouragement and friendship of Heston Blumenthal, who has once again agreed to write the foreword.

Our world's fisheries are mostly in a state of decline, with such a valuable resource disappearing at an horrific rate. Why do we become so fixated on just a few particular species, when simple diversity would enable us not to deplete our valuable supplies? In writing this book I wanted to depict the natural beauty of our oceans through an array of stunning colour photography, whilst making us all aware of the current problems we face in our oceans.

With the help of our sponsors, donations and the sale of the first book, we have started helping others to overcome their troubled times and move forward into a new realm of life.

In the spirit of Dan and from my heart, I thank you.

Kevin

foreword

A Boy after the Sea was a huge success, not only raising money for an extremely worthy cause but also drawing attention to a serious global problem that faces us all. And, as if that wasn't enough, it also won the World's Best Fish and Seafood cookbook at the Gourmand Cookbook Awards in 2010!

The worthy cause is The Dan Snook Trust Foundation which is the charitable organisation Kevin set up in response to his son's tragic death in 2006. The foundation offers a much needed service helping troubled young people who are facing difficult times, often alone and unprotected. Its mission is to transform and enrich the lives of young people who have been victims of sexual or substance abuse and to provide them with the help and support that is so often lacking.

The serious global problem that faces us all is the depletion of the world's fish stocks. Our oceans are under more pressure than ever from human and environmental forces and going forward, well managed and sustainable fishing will be more and more essential for the health of our waters and the livelihoods of those who earn their living from the sea. This book constitutes a fantastic collection of recipes written with these considerations in mind and the range of fish, some familiar and some lesser known, should inspire even the most pessimistic of chefs.

I was delighted to be asked to contribute the foreword to Kevin's second book and, again, it is a huge honour to find myself in such distinguished company. The collection of internationally renowned chefs that he has gathered together is extremely impressive and a great indication of the esteem that Kevin is held in throughout the culinary world. The beautifully shot recipes continue to push the boundaries but will still appeal to cooks of every level.

A Boy after the Sea is a beautiful, inspiring, thought-provoking book and this excellent follow-up won't disappoint. Congratulations, Kevin, you've done it again!

Heston Blumenthal

contents

Grant Achatz

U S A

the plight of the **oceans**

Grant Achatz is the Executive Chef and Co-Owner of Alinea in Chicago, Illinois. In 2010, it was included in San Pellegrino's '50 Best'; Alinea was named as the 'best restaurant in North America' and '7th best in the world'. The James Beard Foundation named Grant 'Outstanding Chef of the Year' in 2008.

Grant was born in St. Clair, Michigan in 1974. After high school, he attended The Culinary Institute of America in Hyde Park, New York, graduating in 1994. In the early years of his career he worked in a handful of professional kitchens, eventually ending up at the French Laundry in Napa Valley, California, with Chef Thomas Keller. Over a four year period, Grant moved up through the French Laundry's kitchen to the role of Keller's Sous-Chef. During this time, he also took a one year hiatus from the kitchen to work as an assistant winemaker at La Jota Vineyards.

In 2001, Grant left the French Laundry to take the role of Executive Chef at Trio, a four-star restaurant in Evanston, Illinois. It was here that Grant began receiving attention and major awards, including the James Beard Foundation's 'Rising Star Chef of the Year' in 2003.

In 2004, Grant left Trio to start planning for his own restaurant with his new business partner, Nick Kokonas. One year later, they opened Alinea in Chicago's Lincoln Park district. Alinea is known throughout the culinary world and Grant its maestro is considered to be one of the edgiest chefs in the world; his work is perceived as having no boundaries.

The name Alinea says it all: in the course of history, an alinea would mark the arrival of a new idea or philosophy – this would often herald the beginning of a new practice or a different way of thinking. Restaurant Alinea situates itself in that sphere, so be prepared – Alinea is a restaurant like no other! ∎

Calculating, controlled and a visionary

Grant Achatz

Photography Lara Kastner

INGREDIENTS: (serves 4)

For the shrimp:
• 4 extra-large shrimp, peeled and deveined

For the preserved Meyer lemon:
• Meyer lemons, quartered, seeds removed
• 160g sugar
• 127g kosher salt

For the cranberry gelée:
• 700g fresh cranberries
• 100g water
• 200g sugar
• 8g agar agar*
• 4 gelatin sheets

For the dry tempura base:
• 100g all-purpose flour
• 12g baking powder
• 15g cornstarch

For the cranberry salt:
• 100g kosher salt
• 100g dried cranberry powder

To assemble and serve:
• 6 whole vanilla beans, one end sharpened to a point
• 150g dry tempura base
• 300g cold sparkling water, preferably highly carbonated
• 50g all-purpose flour
• 1000g canola oil

*   *Agar agar is a gelatinous substance derived from seaweed.*
** *Chinois is a fine conical strainer.*

shrimp with lemon and cranberry

with vanilla fragrance

PREPARATION:

Shrimp – cut the shrimp into three 2.5cm pieces and keep to one side. Discard the 2.5cm tail pieces.

Preserved Meyer lemon – in a large bowl combine lemons, sugar and salt and stir to coat. Transfer coated lemons and any remaining sugar and salt to an airtight container. Freeze mixture, covered, for 3 months. Remove frozen lemons and rinse well in cold water. Using a vegetable peeler, remove rind. Remove and discard flesh and pith from rind. Cut rind into 1.3cm squares.

Cranberry gelée – line a 22.9cm by 30.5cm pan with plastic wrap. In a large vacuum bag combine cranberries, water and sugar and seal on high setting. Cook en sous-vide in a large pot of water at 95°C for 30 minutes. Immerse gelatin sheets in a bowl of ice water for 5 minutes, or until pliable. Remove the sheets and squeeze out excess water. Transfer cranberry mixture to blender and blend on high speed for 2 minutes, or until smooth. Strain through a chinois** and transfer to a clean saucepan. Add agar agar and place back over high heat. Bring to a simmer and cook for 2 minutes. Add gelatin sheets and stir to dissolve. Strain through the chinois into the prepared pan and refrigerate, taking care to keep it level, for about 45 minutes, or until gelée is firm. Cut into 1.3cm cubes and keep in the refrigerator.

Dry tempura base – in a small bowl stir together the flour, baking powder and cornstarch. Transfer to an airtight container. Reserve.

Cranberry salt – in a small bowl stir together the cranberry powder and kosher salt. Transfer to an airtight container. Reserve.

Finishing and presentation – heat oil to 191°C in a large, heavy pot. Using the sharpened end, skewer ingredients on vanilla bean in the following order, leaving no space between them: one lemon rind square, one cranberry gelée square, and one piece of shrimp. Position ingredients so that rind sits about 7.6cm from the end of the skewer and the shrimp sits flush with tip of the bean.

Dip the skewered ingredients in the flour and tap off any excess. Dip in tempura batter. Immerse battered end in oil just to cover, and fry for 2 minutes. Drain briefly on paper towels, sprinkle with cranberry salt, and serve. ■

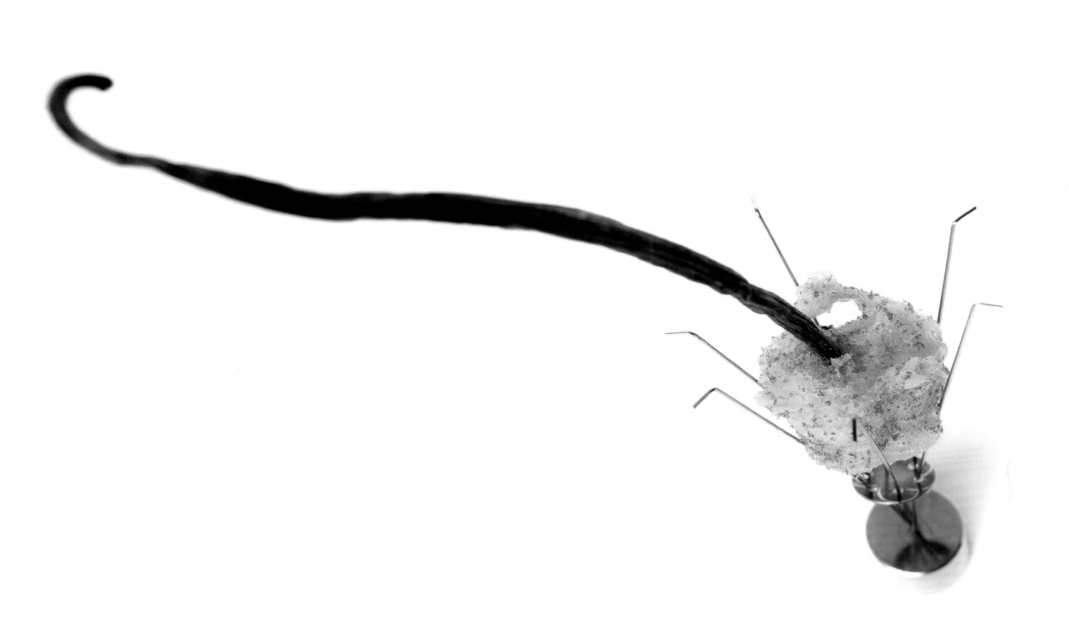

15

The plight of the oceans

Oceans are literally the source of life on earth. They shape the climate, feed the world, and cleanse the air that we breathe. However, the marine ecosystem exists as a finely balanced set of interdependent relationships between organisms and is thus highly susceptible to disruption and intervention.

Currently the earth's oceans and their inhabitants are being threatened by a dizzying array of dangers, from piracy to climate change to overfishing. States have the legal right to regulate fishing in their exclusive economic zones (EEZs), which extend two hundred nautical miles from shore. But outside these boundaries lie the high seas, which are free from any one country's jurisdiction. The precept of 'Freedom of the Seas' is critical to the free flow of global commerce, but has spelt disaster for international fisheries and is yielding a tragedy of epic proportions. For years, large-scale fishing vessels have harvested fish as fast as they could, with minimal regulation, killing a staggering 90% of the ocean's large commercial species in just one century.

2

Massimiliano Alajmo

ITALY

devastation of
the deep

Born in Padua, Italy, in 1974, Chef Massimiliano Alajmo is a part of the fifth generation of the family to work in the world of food, alongside his brother Raffaele and sister Laura. After graduating from the College of Hotel Management Pietro d'Abano in 1993, he did his formal training in the kitchens of Alfredo Chiochetti's restaurant 'Ja Navalge' in Moena. He also cooked alongside famous chefs such as Marc Veyrat and Michel Guérard, before taking over as the Executive Chef of 'Le Calandre' in 1994. The restaurant had already gained one-Michelin-star, poignantly awarded to Massimiliano's mother Rita Chimetto in 1992. The restaurant received its second star under the guidance of this dynamic chef just four years later, making Massimiliano the youngest chef to receive the honour. In the same year he was described as 'the Mozart of cookery' by food critic Paolo Marchi. The third star was achieved in November 2002, once again making him the youngest chef ever to obtain such an accolade.

In 2004 Raffaele, Massimiliano and the Alajmo family opened Il Calandrino, a relaxed restaurant located next door to Le Calandre where guests could enjoy meals throughout the day. Since that time the brothers have written their first cookery book, 'In.gredienti', which was named 'Best Cookbook in the World 2007' at the famous Gourmand International World Cookbook Awards.

The family has also opened a successful gourmet food shop in Tokyo, designed and produced their own line of tableware, and also worked closely with a famous perfumer called Lorenzo Dante Ferro researching the sense of smell; this has led to the production of a line of essential oils, used on dishes and cocktails to stimulate the senses.

Today the Alajmo family owns and manages three restaurants, as well as the Gourmet food store and a small boutique hotel called 'Maccaroni'. They also work closely with a non-profit organisation raising large sums of money to support the research of infant diseases.

Now known as Italy's most famous three-Michelin-star chef, Massimiliano Alajmo is revered by clients and peers alike for his unique interpretation and elaboration of traditional Italian cuisine. ∎

Inspiring Italy's new generation

Massimiliano Alajmo

Photography Mario Reggiani

cuttlefish cappuccino

INGREDIENTS: (serves 6)

For the cuttlefish in its ink:
- 450g cleaned cuttlefish, cut into small cubes
- 225g vegetable gelatin broth
- 45g white wine
- 30g white onion, minced
- 30g extra virgin olive oil
- $1/6$th garlic clove
- $1/3$rd bay leaf
- Pinch of salt
- Cuttlefish ink (removed from sack while cleaning cuttlefish)

For the potato cream:
- 675g white potato, peeled and cut into 2cm cubes
- 150g fresh heavy cream
- 145g whole milk
- 90g boiling vegetable gelatin broth
- 30g extra virgin olive oil
- 9g salt
- 4.5g castor sugar
- 4.5g chives, minced
- 2.5g soy sauce

Finishing:
- $1^1/_2$ tsp chives, finely chopped
- A few drops of extra virgin olive oil

PREPARATION:

Cuttlefish in its ink – sweat the onion and garlic in the extra virgin oil, add cuttlefish, brown slightly and add white wine a little at a time. Evaporate liquid then add cuttlefish ink and the vegetable gelatin broth gradually. Cover and cook slowly until cuttlefish is tender.

Potato cream – boil potatoes in a large pot of unsalted water. Blend in Thermomix* at 60°C adding milk, heavy cream, soy sauce, sugar and salt. Drizzle in extra virgin and emulsify with boiling broth. Pour cream in a hot terrine, add chives and mix delicately.

Finishing and presentation – place a tablespoon of cuttlefish in its ink in a transparent glass and cover with potato cream. Garnish with a few drops of cooking juice and extra virgin; sprinkle with a pinch of chive.

Parsley stock – blend all the ingredients together, strain and season. ■

HINTS – based on potato type, the quantities of other ingredients may vary (for example, potatoes with more starch may need additional liquid).

VARIATIONS – serve hot potato cream with a white seafood stew of red mullet, spider crab, various kinds of shrimp, manila clams, mussels and their cooking juices sprinkled with nigella** seed-infused olive oil, roughly chopped parsley and hot chilli pepper powder.

---

* *Thermomix is a super-fast food blender and processor that also weighs, cooks, simmers and steams!*

** *Nigella is a tiny black seed, similar to a poppy seed, popular in Indian cooking and is often used to make chutney and pickles.*

Devastation of the deep

The world's seas have always been farmed for protein rich seafood but its bounty from the deep blue expanse of the ocean – the last frontier – is not as inexhaustible as it once seemed.

Technology has now given humanity the ability to harvest at will; we can now fish anywhere, at any depth, for any species. To feed a growing world population with a rapacious appetite by using unchecked and unrestrained methods has been calamitous for many fish stocks and the sustainability of their very existence is now severely threatened. The most destructive of these practices is the use of drift nets that create 'walls of death' for all but the smallest sea creatures. However, drift nets are not the only source of indiscriminate fishing.

Nets kill cetaceans, longline use kills birds, bottom trawlers obliterate ecosystems. Furthermore, unscrupulous and irresponsible fishermen have a strong economic incentive to ply their trade because many species of fish, particularly those which have been already over-exploited and are thus in short supply, are of high value. This situation is allowed to flourish because of the failure of governments to either regulate their seas adequately or to enforce national or international laws either because of lack of capacity, indifference or undue political influence of large sections of the fishing industry and their representatives.

3

Juan Mari & Elena Arzak

SPAIN

overfishing

The genius of Arzak is that it has been reaching for the stars for more than three decades. It was the first restaurant in Spain to be awarded three-Michelin-stars in 1989, and since then it has kept its feet firmly on the ground, honouring the culinary traditions and the rich soil of the Basque country. Despite its celebrity following and cutting edge cuisine, Arzak retains the charm and unpretentiousness of a family restaurant, allowing you to immediately feel at home when you walk through its doors.

The restaurant has been in the Arzak family since the house was built in 1987, when it was opened as a bodega on the outskirts of San Sebastian by Escolastica; she was the grandmother of the current owner Juan Mari Arzak, who now runs the restaurant with his daughter Elena. Together they manage a highly professional team. Through tremendous enthusiasm, dedication and drive they produce some truly incredible dishes from the stoves of this fine restaurant.

One of the Arzak's best kept secrets is the experimentation in the kitchen, where flavours, textures and processes are utilised; this means the restaurant evolves every day, through the creativity and inspiration of the team. Juan Mari and Elena lead this group of alchemists that try in deciphering the secrets of the culinary arts. Their biggest challenge is to find the perfect balance between the avant-garde and the roots of tradition. This important work is carried out in a quiet place equipped with the latest facilities – besides the experimental kitchen there is a 'flavour bank' that contains more than 1400 products and ingredients, for use in the discovery of new creations.

As one critic says, "Arzak's cuisine goes far beyond surprising – it is endlessly rewarding. It offers its customers a beautiful play of flavours, textures and temperatures that involve all senses like no other cuisine I have ever tried." ■

A family revolutionising Basque cuisine

Juan Mari & Elena Arzak

INGREDIENTS: (serves 4)

For the chipirón:
- 1 x 700g large chipirón (Begi Haundi – squid)
- 8g orange zest, dried
- 1tbsp chopped parsley
- 25g garlic oil
- Salt
- Powdered ginger and Sarsaparilla powder to taste**

For the squid sand:
- 100g squid
- 1tsp olive oil

For the squid sauce:
- 300g cuttlefish using the sepia ink
- 1 onion
- 2 green peppers
- 1 garlic clove
- 1 small tomato
- 25g olive oil
- ½ glass red wine
- 2.5kg water
- Salt to taste

For the round ink pearls:
- 1kg water
- 5g alginate*
- 250g squid ink sauce
- 3.5g glucose
- 100g sunflower oil

For the red mushrooms:
- 50g white mushrooms
- 200g beetroot juice
- 1tbsp olive oil
- Salt

For the onion broth:
- 3 onions
- 100g water
- 1tsp lavender
- Salt and pepper

For the enokis:
- 80g enokis***
- 2tbsp garlic oil
- Salt

tender young squid

with ink pearls, red mushrooms, enokis and onion broth

PREPARATION:

The chipirón – clean the chipiróns and separate on one side the fins and the legs, from the bodies. Take the bodies and open them in half. Once opened, cut them into squares and make several incisions without going right through. Marinate for 12 hours with the garlic oil, salt, ginger, parsley and Sarsaparilla powder. Cook the chipiróns on a large cast iron pan until nice and coloured. Cover them with the chopped parsley.

Squid sand – cut the squid and sauté with the oil, allow to cool. Place in a dryer which will take approximately 36 hours in order to complete the process. Once dried, make it into a powder by placing it in a food processor. Keep in a sous-vide bag.

Squid sauce – cut the onion, pepper and garlic all into julienne – submerge everything in the oil. Clean the cuttlefish and separate the ink. Cut all of the meat into pieces, making sure that they are not too small. Once the vegetables are ready, add the meat. Then add the rest of the liquid, add the wine and then reduce, add the ink diluted in the water. Mix everything and cover with water. Allow to cook for 30 minutes over a medium heat. Separate the meat and blitz the rest, strain and season.

Round ink pearls – dissolve the glucose in the squid ink sauce. Blitz both ingredients and keep refrigerated for 1 hour in order to eliminate the excess air. Set aside. Mix the alginate with the water and allow to stand for 6 hours. Reserve. Add drops of the black sauce into the alginate and water solution. It is very important that the drops do not touch themselves. Allow to stand in the solution for 3 minutes. Strain with a slotted spoon and clean in fresh water. Keep them in the sunflower oil until needed.

Red mushrooms – cut the mushrooms and marinate for 1 hour in the beet juice. Strain the mushrooms and lightly sauté in a hot pan and season.

Onion broth – bake the onions with their skins at 180°C for 50 minutes. Peel them, add the lavender and water. Place in a sous-vide bag and cook for 2 hours at 65°C. Strain and season.

The enokis – sauté them lightly in the oil and season.

Finishing and presentation – place the two fillets of chipirón in the centre of the plate, sprinkle with sand. Place the round ink pearls, the red mushrooms and the enokis next to them. Serve with the onion broth. ∎

* *Algin is a natural product extracted from brown algae that grow in cold water regions, as a refined powder algin gels in the presence of calcic. It dilutes while cold with strong agitation, it need not be heated to produce spherification.*

** *Sarsaparilla powder, sometimes called beer root, produces a strong aroma and flavour and is often used as a tea or beverage.*

*** *Enokis – a mushroom with a long thin stem in the genus Flammulina, used primarily in the cuisines of East Asia.*

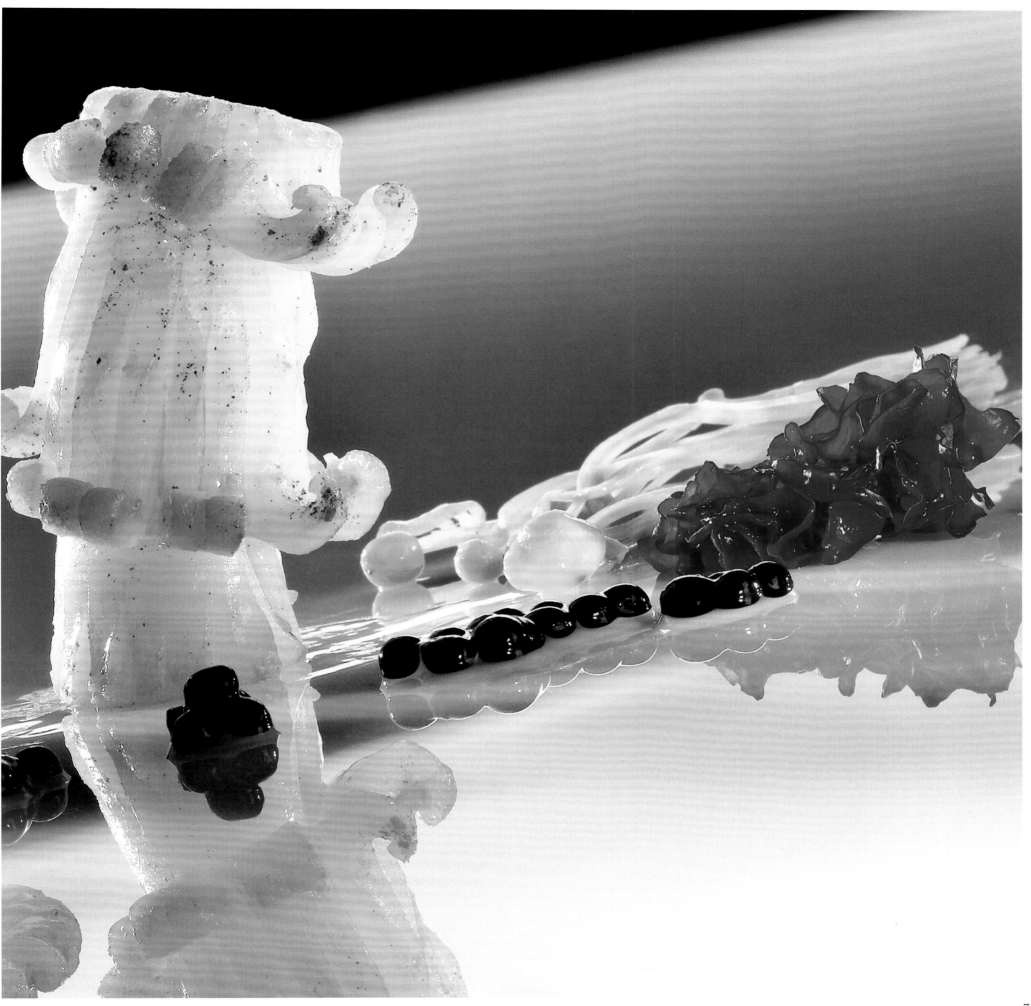

Overfishing

Overfishing is the number one problem facing the world's oceans. Formally defined as "situations where one or more fish stocks are reduced below predefined levels of acceptance by fishing activities", overfishing occurs when fish stocks are depleted to the point where they may not be able to recover. Areas such as the eastern coast of Canada and the northeastern coast of the U.S. have fished certain species to collapse, which consequently caused the fishing communities that relied on those stocks to fold.

In some cases, depleted fish stocks have been restored; however, this is only possible when the species' ecosystem remains intact. If the species depletion causes an imbalance in the ecosystem, not only is it difficult for the depleted stocks to return to sustainable levels, other species dependent on the depleted stocks may become imbalanced themselves, causing further problems. In a self-perpetuating manner, the more fish stocks become overexploited, the more fisheries must search for productive waters that in turn are then quickly depleted also. Writing in the journal Science, the international team of researchers say that there will be virtually nothing left to fish from the seas by the middle of the century if current trends continue. One of the scientists on the project added: "Unless we fundamentally change the way we manage all the ocean species together, as working ecosystems, then this century is the last century of wild seafood."

4

José Avillez
PORTUGAL

illegal, unregulated and
unreported

José Avillez is considered to be one of the icons of Portuguese cuisine. He wanted to be a chef from early childhood, and his dream came true after finishing a degree in business communication and marketing, with a final thesis on Portuguese gastronomy. His culinary journey began at 'Fortaleza do Guincho', one of the best hotels in Cascais, after which he worked with José Bento dos Santos in Quinta do Monte d'Oiro, which led to the opportunity of professional culinary sessions with Maria de Lourdes Modesto. José then travelled a great deal, training, working and studying in some of the greatest kitchens in the world. Names such as Alain Ducasse, Ferran Adrià, Claude Troisgros and Eric Frechon have all influenced and inspired his work. His work has always stood out for the strictness of his technique, and for an insatiable desire to create and always go further beyond.

A young, dynamic, insatiable creator

In 2005, José Avillez was awarded the 'Chef d'Avenir' prize, by the international Academy of Gastronomy. In 2008, before reaching 30 years of age, José was invited to take the helm at the Old Tavares Rico, Portugal's oldest and most exclusive restaurant. He has managed to revive this restaurant, bringing to it a new sophisticated cuisine that still remains loyal to the natural tastes and styles of Portuguese tradition. In 2009 his dedication paid off with the honour of being awarded a Michelin-star.

Other achievements include being the first Portuguese chef to be invited to participate in 'Madrid Fusión', the greatest and most notorious cuisine congress worldwide.

Apart from his restaurant business this young and dynamic chef writes cookery books, teaches cookery, caters for private clients and now provides a 'takeaway' service! He has achieved culinary stardom in Portugal and beyond! ■

José Avillez

INGREDIENTS: (serves 6)

For the red mullet:
- 3 x 300g red mullets

For the charcoal powder:
- 100g of breadcrumbs, cuttlefish ink, smoke powder

For the red mullet stock (250ml):
- Bones of 3 red mullets
- 50g shallots, 30g of leeks, both julienned
- 40g ripe tomato, peeled, seeded and diced, 20g tomato pulp
- 20ml white wine, 50ml olive oil, 300ml mineral water

For the 'migas' embers:
- 20g minced garlic
- 100ml olive oil
- 500ml striped red mullet stock
- 300g corn bread
- 30g cuttlefish ink, salt to taste

For the charcoal olive oil:
- 100g charcoal, 200ml olive oil

For the rosemary infusion:
- 500ml mineral water and 70g fresh rosemary

For the rosemary meringue:
- 8 gelatin sheets
- 470ml of rosemary infusion
- 2.5g methylcellulose***
- 8g salt, 5g cuttlefish ink

For the edible branches:
- 96g flour, 3g yeast, 57g milk
- Cuttlefish ink, 1.5g salt

For the red mullet liver sauce:
- Liver of 2 red mullets, 100ml red mullet stock
- 10g shallots
- 10ml olive oil, 15g butter, lemon juice, sea salt

To serve:
- Scales of black salt, black salt powder
- Olive oil, Pop Rocks*

* *Pop Rocks – a carbonated candy that creates a fizzy reaction when it dissolves in the mouth.*
** *Chinois see p14.*
*** *Methylcellulose is a chemical compound derived from cellulose, in its powder form it dissolves in cold water, forming a clear viscous gel and is used as a thickener and an emulsifier.*

roast red mullet on a beach fire with 'migas' embers

with cuttlefish ink and liver sauce

PREPARATION:

Red mullet – scale and wash the red mullets, setting the livers aside. Fillet and remove the bones with tweezers. Chill. Use the bones and heads to make the stock.

Charcoal powder – cut bread into pieces, colour with cuttlefish ink, water and pinch of smoke powder. Place in oven (pre-heated 160°C) for 7 minutes until crunchy. Cool, reduce to powder in coffee mill.

Red mullet stock – brown fish bones on both sides, in very hot olive oil. Add vegetables and caramelize slightly, add tomato pulp, freshen up with white wine and let evaporate. Add mineral water, 150ml for every 100g of bones, simmer for 15 minutes. Strain and cool quickly. Chill.

'Migas' embers – cut the bread into small cubes and cover with part of the red mullet stock. In a pan, sauté the minced garlic with the olive oil and add the bread. Let it cook; add some more stock and the cuttlefish ink. Season with salt. It is ready when it starts to form a ball.

Charcoal olive oil – in an iron pan over a strong fire, char the charcoal until it turns to embers. Let it cool, place it in a vessel, add the olive oil, cover it with foil and chill for 24 hours in a dry place before using it. Strain through a chinois** and keep the olive oil in an adequate bottle (always use moderately).

For the rosemary infusion – place rosemary and water in a vacuum bag, seal and make an infusion keeping it in a 65°C bain marie for 1 hour.

Rosemary meringue – soften gelatin in cold water and melt over a low heat. Mix methylcellulose, rosemary infusion and cuttlefish ink. Salt and stir. Add melted gelatin and stir. Cover, chill in refrigerator.

Edible branches – mix all the ingredients, except the salt. Stir in a kitchen mixer medium speed, for 4 minutes. Add the salt, stir for 1 minute more. Work the dough with your hands for 5 minutes. Roll it in a wet cloth and let it chill in the refrigerator for at least 3 hours before using. Take small pieces of the dough and roll them into a branch shape. Place them in the oven, heated to 160°C, for 7 minutes.

Red mullet liver sauce – sauté the finely chopped shallot with the olive oil, without browning. Add the livers and mash them with a fork, let it caramelize slightly. Add the striped red mullet stock (100ml of stock for each 2 livers), bring it to a boil, and stir. Strain through a fine strainer and re-heat. Reduce until the sauce gains texture. Season with salt, add a splash of lemon juice and knob of butter.

Finishing and presentation – season red mullet with black salt powder and splash of olive oil. Cook in oven or a salamander stove until slightly cooked. Stir rosemary meringue in kitchen mixer, on maximum power for first minute, then finish with medium speed. Place charcoal powder, 'migas', the red mullet, rosemary meringue and branches on a plate. Finish with scales of black salt, liver sauce, and right before serving sprinkle the fizzy Pop Rocks on the liver sauce. Reacting with the hot and moist sauce they will start fizzing, reminding us the embers of a bonfire. Serve immediately. ■

Illegal, unregulated and unreported

Respecting neither national boundaries nor international attempts to manage high seas resources, illegal, unreported and unregulated (IUU) fishing is a serious global problem that continues to grow at an alarming rate.

Illegal fishing takes place where vessels operate in violation of the laws of a fishery. This can apply to fisheries that are under the jurisdiction of a coastal state or to high seas fisheries regulated by regional organisations.

Unreported fishing is fishing that has been unreported or misreported to the relevant national authority or regional organisation, in contravention of applicable laws and regulations.

Unregulated fishing generally refers to fishing by vessels without nationality, or vessels flying the flag of a country not party to the regional organisation governing that fishing area or species.

IUU fishing thrives particularly where weak governance arrangements prevail and is further encouraged by the failure of some countries to meet their international responsibilities. It puts unsustainable pressure on fish stocks, marine wildlife and habitats.

Reaching for the stars

Claude Bosi was born in Lyon into a family of restaurateurs. He completed his apprenticeship in his home town before moving to Paris, where he trained under some of the greatest chefs in France – most notably Alain Passard, Alain Ducasse and Jean-Paul Lacombe. Having gained so much experience working with these true masters, he left his home country in 1997 to work in England, and to pursue his goal of establishing his own restaurant. In 2000 'Hibiscus' opened in Ludlow, Shropshire, and was soon awarded its first Michelin-star; its second star followed just three years later. In 2007 Claude Bosi and his wife Claire relocated their two-Michelin-starred 'Hibiscus' restaurant from Ludlow to London.

Bosi's powerful modern French cuisine – with its bold and surprising combination of flavours – soon became recognised as one of London's most sought after dining experiences. He continues to receive many accolades for his unique talent of producing dishes of ingenuity and originality. In 2010 Hibiscus entered the S. Pellegrino World's 50 Best Restaurants list at number 49 – one of only three British restaurants on the list. ■

Claude Bosi

soused Cornish
line caught mackerel

with Yorkshire rhubarb, button mushrooms
& white miso

INGREDIENTS: (serves 4)

- 2 x 200g mackerel fillets
- 200g button mushrooms
- 100g dashi
- Arrow root
- Salt
- Sugar
- ½ litre rice vinegar
- 50g teriyaki sauce
- 4 sticks of rhubarb
- 1 bunch dill
- 200g vegetable oil

For the mushroom soup:
- 200g smoked mackerel
- 200g button mushrooms
- 100g dashi
- Yuzu
- Salt

PREPARATION:

Mackerel – souse the mackerel fillet for 1 minute in rice vinegar. Remove the film from the skin and marinate for 30 minutes in the vinegar. Take out the liquid and pin-bone the mackerel. Just before serving, smear the mackerel with teriyaki sauce.

Rhubarb – peel 4 sticks of rhubarb. Make a solution of $1/3$ sugar and $2/3$ water. Immerse peelings for 10 seconds. Strain through a sieve and chill. Put the rhubarb sticks in a bag with the poaching syrup for approximately 20 minutes or until very soft. Cut equal sized rectangles. Set aside. Bring the vinegar marinade to the boil. Add arrow root, pinch by pinch, until a liquid consistency is reached.

Mushroom soup – blitz all ingredients together. Strain. Pour into the bottom of a demitasse cup. Blend miso and water together. Coat the mushroom soup to finish.

Dill oil – blanch the dill for 15 seconds. Refresh in iced water. Press to remove the water. Blitz with vegetable oil to correct consistency and add salt.

Finishing and presentation – arrange the mackerel and the rhubarb on your designated plate and garnish with dill oil and dill shoots. Accompany with the mushroom miso soup. ■

Drift nets

Perhaps the most pernicious of fishing methods is the use of drift nets, which are used in almost every ocean, mainly in the Pacific and Atlantic, as well as in many seas such as the Mediterranean.

Drift nets get their name from the manner in which they are worked. The nets are cast or shot into the sea where they hang perpendicularly from floats on the surface of the sea, forming, as it were, a perforated wall. When the shoals of fish try to pass through the perforations or meshes, they are caught because the meshes are only large enough to permit the head and the gills of the fish to enter, but too small to allow the thicker part of the body of the fish to pass through. Stretching across the ocean at over 50 km in length, a drift net hangs like a giant veil of death in the sea.

There are three main problems with the use of drift nets: ghost fishing, drop-out and bycatch.

6

Massimo Bottura
ITALY

ghost fishing

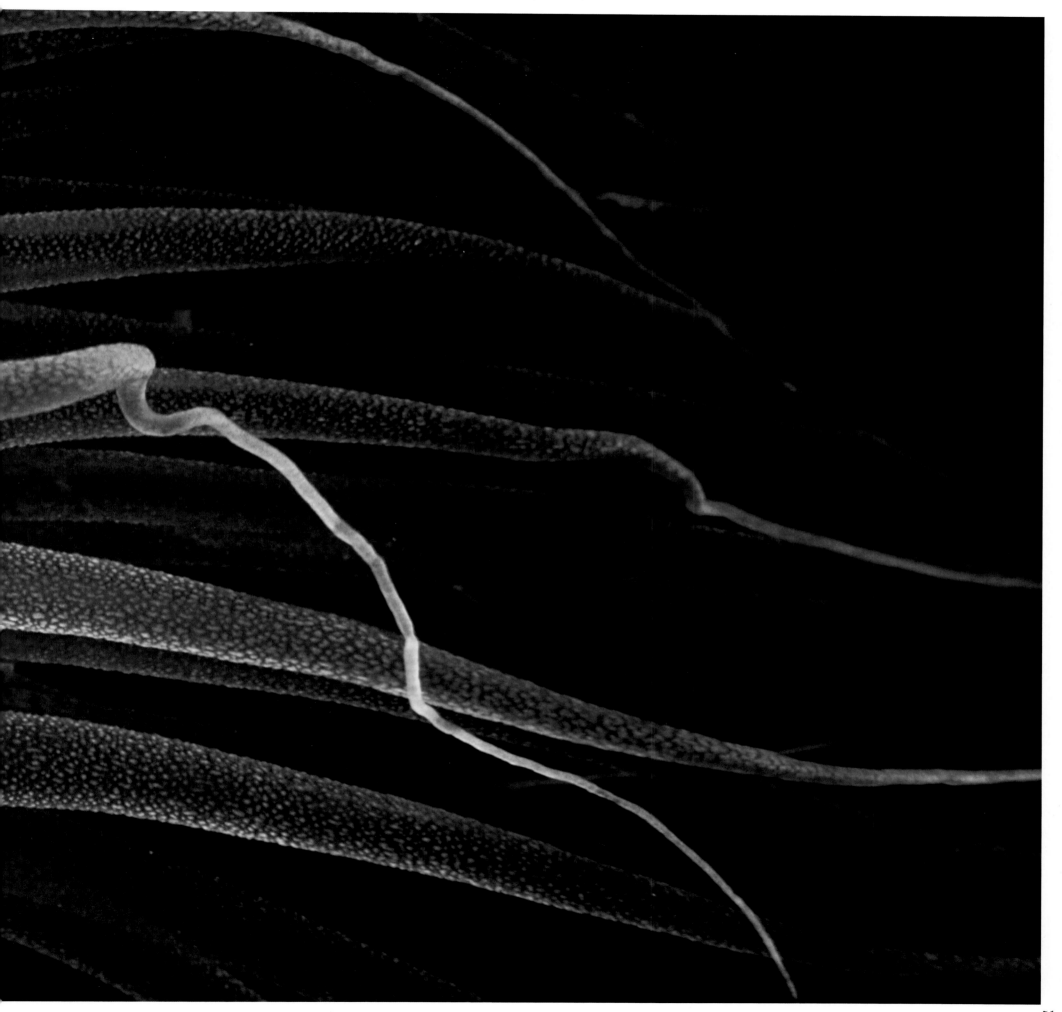

An artist with food, a musician, a lover of poetry and a perfectionist!

'Evolution, not revolution, is the way forward for modern Italian food' says Chef Massimo Bottura, a key figure amongst the new generation of avant-garde chefs, to be recognised not only as chefs, but as artists both in and out of their kitchens.

Bottura has gained much recognition in the international 'gastro communities' and also among artists and art lovers. He is a man who appreciates art, music, history and poetry, all influences of which ensure his perfection within his own craft. His restaurant, Osteria Francescana, is in Modena, lying in the heart of the Emilia Romagna region of Italy. It is the holder of a coveted two-Michelin-stars and in 2010 it was rated number six in the world at the San Pellegrino Awards.

Massimo strongly believes that innovation is the foundation of tradition. He describes his kitchen as 'territorial cuisine' seen from some 10 kilometres away! In fact Bottura invites surprise by breaking the rules, offering unexpected combinations of familiar ingredients in a minimalist setting surrounded by contemporary art and Italian design.

When asked where his food inspirations come from he quotes Alain Ducasse, Ferran Adrià and reinventing the cuisine of his grandmother. ∎

Massimo Bottura

INGREDIENTS: (serves 4)

For the fish:
- 60 rossetti (whitebait from red mullets)
- 6 red shrimp
- 1 small mackerel
- 6 small bay scallops
- 50g amberjack belly
- 3 scampi
- 6 cooked mussels

For the vegetables: (quantities as desired)
- Daikon
- Red seaweed
- Sea lettuce
- Oyster leaves
- Parsley
- Garlic
- Lemon juice
- White fish fat
- Mussel water (from cooked mussels)
- Lecithin
- 2 large oysters
- Oyster water (place oysters and their water aside)
- Cervia sea salt
- Lemon leaves (process in a volcano vaporizer*
  to achieve smoke)

The volcano vaporizer is used in kitchens as a method of applying controlled heat to foods, herbs and spices to release flavours that otherwise would be difficult to titrate or apply, used primarily in molecular gastronomy.

'Adriatic fish market'

a portrait of our fish markets in the Adriatic Sea

PREPARATION:

Fish – clean thoroughly all of the fish and cut into small pieces.

Vegetables – julienne the daikon finely. Tear red seaweed and the sea lettuce and marinate in mussel water (water from cooked mussels), lemon juice, pinch of sugar and salt for 2 hours.

Fish fat – prepare an infusion of bones and fish scraps with spring water. Infuse at 60°C for 12 hours. Clean any brine off the top surface. Filter the infusion into a tall, thin container and bring to 3°C in a flash freezer. Separate the pure fat on the upper layer from the liquid below. Warm the fat and filter. Conserve at 5°C.

Frozen sheet of oyster water – fill a shallow bowl with spring water 5mm from the border. Place in a flash freezer (-18°C) for 5 minutes or until the water forms a thin layer of ice. Gently pierce the ice and let out the excess water, keeping the ice layer intact and in place. Pour a thin layer of oyster water over the ice sheet and place in a flash freezer for 2 hours. Keep frozen until ready to serve.

Oyster cream – purée the raw oysters adding oyster water and blending into a smooth cream.

Lemon and fish fat emulsion – add chilled fresh lemon juice slowly to the fish fat whipping the mixture constantly. Keep blending until the texture is similar to mayonnaise.

Parsley mayonnaise – blanch the parsley in spring water for a few seconds then immediately place in ice water. Blend the parsley with cold mineral water for 2 minutes at the highest speed. Filter. Add mussel water and a clove of blanched garlic. Blend and filter again. Add salt and place in a stainless steel container. Slowly add the olive oil and a touch of lecithin until the mixture becomes a green vegetable mayonnaise.

Finishing and presentation – insert a $1/6$ th of the oyster purée into the tiny hole in the ice. Inject lemon leaf smoke into the hole. Place all the raw fish, oyster leaves, marinated vegetables, lemon emulsion, fresh lemon zest and several granules of sweet Cervia salt on top of the frozen oyster water. Smoke lightly on the surface and serve immediately. Break the ice to release the smoke. Spoon from the bottom up, mixing the elements as you go. ■

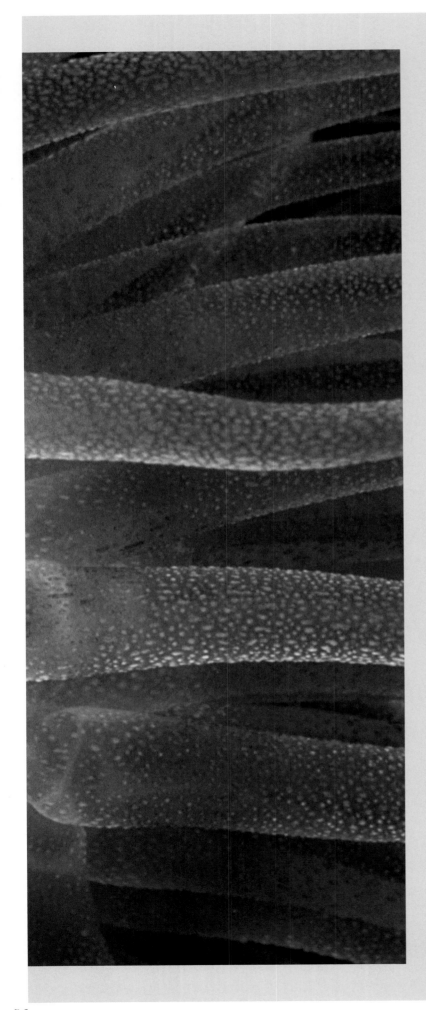

Ghost fishing

Ghost fishing occurs when a drift net, often made of non-biodegradable plastic or nylon, breaks loose on its own and is free to sail the ocean. When a net is free-floating like this it is moved by winds and currents all over the ocean. It becomes an invisible death trap, killing whatever it touches. It will continue to do this until the weight of the creatures it has ensnared finally drags it to the bottom or it washes ashore.

Any abandoned, lost or otherwise discarded fishing gear can, in fact, induce ghost fishing but for every drift net fleet it is estimated that 1,000 km of ghost net is left in the ocean, enough to stretch ½ of the way around the earth and constituting about 10% of marine litter.

Daniel Boulud
U S A

bycatch

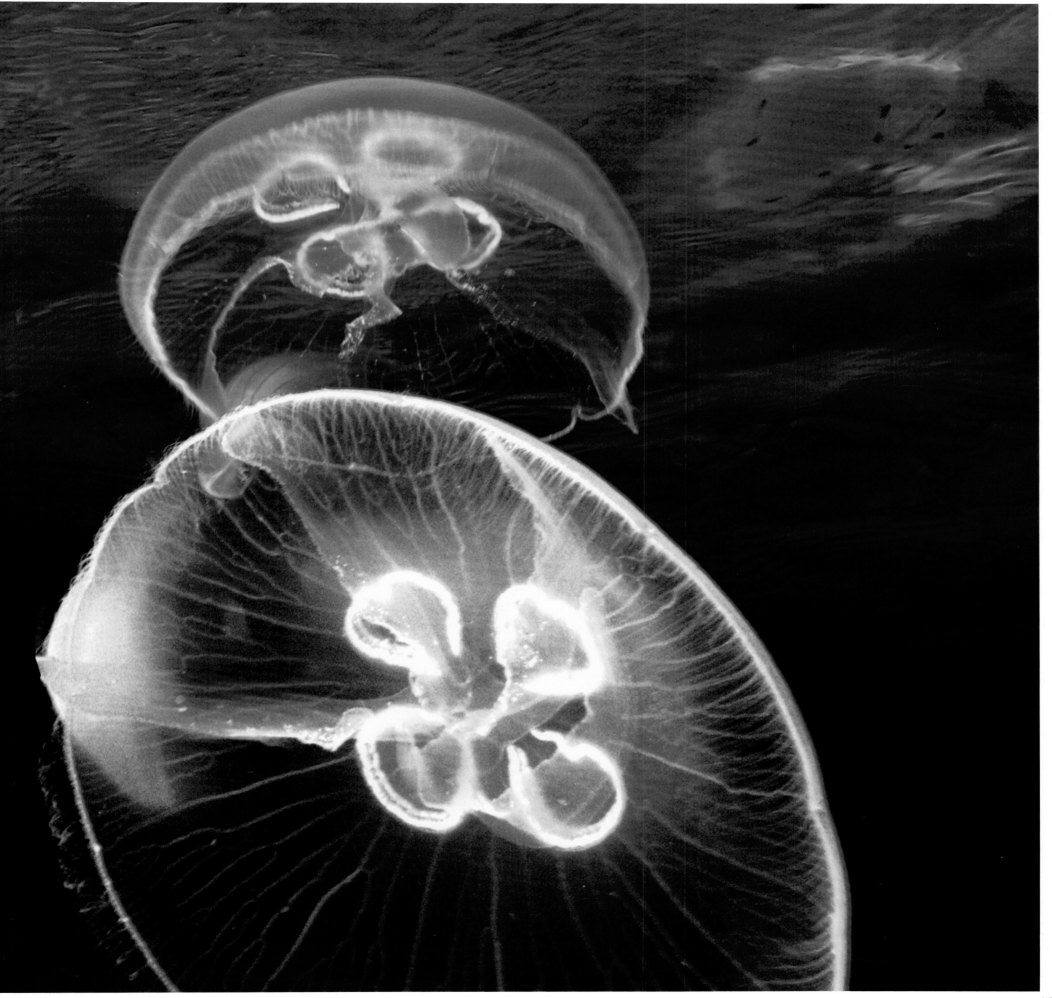

Daniel Boulud is Chef-Owner of several award-winning restaurants, as well as the Feast & Fêtes catering company. While he originates from Lyon, France, it was in New York that he truly conquered the dining scene, and today he is considered one of America's leading culinary authorities. Raised on his family's farm in the village of St. Pierre de Chandieu, the chef remains inspired by the rhythm of the seasons, and menus driven by quality ingredients. Since arriving in the United States in 1982, Chef Boulud has become renowned for the contemporary appeal he adds to soulful cooking rooted in French tradition.

His New York City restaurants include Daniel, a three-Michelin-star Relais & Châteaux member; the elegant Café Boulud with its adjacent new Bar Pleiades; DB Bistro Moderne; Bar Boulud and most recently DBGB Kitchen and Bar. Beyond Manhattan he has created Café Boulud in Palm Beach, Florida, and will add a new DB Bistro Moderne in downtown Miami in October 2010. The chef has extended his culinary reach internationally with Maison Boulud in Beijing's Legation Quarter, as well as Vancouver's DB Bistro Moderne, and the renowned Relais & Château restaurant, Lumière. 2010 will also see the opening of a new DB Bistro Moderne to Singapore's Marina Bay Sands Resort, and the opening of his first restaurant in the UK at London's Mandarin Oriental.

Boulud's culinary accolades include James Beard Foundation awards for 'Outstanding Restaurateur,' 'Best Chef of New York City' and 'Outstanding Chef of the Year'. In addition, he has been named a Chevalier de la Légion d'Honneur by the French government. Restaurant Daniel has been cited as "one of the ten best restaurants in the world" by the International Herald Tribune, earned a coveted four-star rating from the New York Times, and Wine Spectator's 'Grand Award'. Daniel was also voted the highest climber in the San Pellegrino Awards for 2010, taking the number eight position.

Despite being one of the best chefs in the world, Daniel is a warm friendly character with a very generous nature. He is an inspiration to young chefs and often keeps a watchful eye over their chosen career paths! ■

From farm to fame

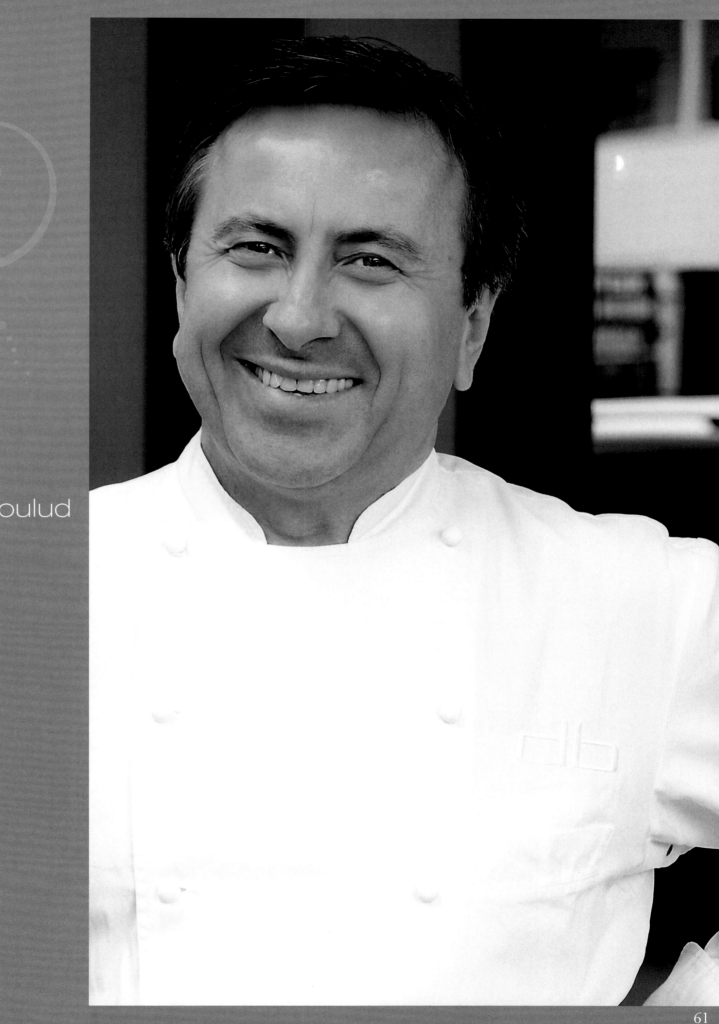

Daniel Boulud

INGREDIENTS: (serves 6)

For the slow-baked striped bass:
- 1 whole striped bass, about 6.8kg filleted, skinned and bones removed
- Olive oil, juice of 1 lemon
- Salt and pepper
- Cilantro pistou (recipe follows)

For the cilantro pistou:
- 1 bunch fresh cilantro, leaves only, washed and roughly chopped
- 2tbsp toasted pine nuts
- 240ml olive oil
- Salt and ground white pepper

For the artichoke barigoule:
- 2tsp coriander
- ¼tsp chilli flakes
- 1 fresh bay leaf, 2 sprigs thyme
- 560ml chicken stock
- 60ml fresh lemon juice, 240ml olive oil
- 4 large artichokes
- Salt and pepper

For the sauce:
- 480ml chicken stock
- 2tbsp tapioca pearls
- 560ml reduced artichoke cooking liquid (see above)
- 2tbsp Dijon mustard, 120ml olive oil
- ½ bunch fresh cilantro, leaves only, thinly sliced

For the lemon arancini (makes about 30 pieces)
- 1.8 litres unsalted chicken broth
- 8tbsp (1 stick) butter
- 1 small onion, peeled and diced
- 450g arborio rice
- Salt and freshly ground pepper
- 113g Parmesan cheese, grated, 1tbsp mascarpone cheese
- Finely grated zest of 1 lemon, 113ml fresh lemon juice
- Salt and freshly ground black pepper
- 113g cornstarch or as needed
- Vegetable oil for frying

To serve
- 450g fava beans, boiled and shelled
- 450g raw artichokes, peeled
- 56g each micro cilantro and chickpea tendrils (available at chefs-garden.com)
- fresh lemon juice, olive oil

slow-baked striped bass

artichokes barigoule, lemon arancini and cilantro pistou

PREPARATION:

Slow-baked striped bass – heat the oven to 200°C. Trim bloodline from fish. Divide into 6 rectangular portions about 125-135g each. Season all sides with olive oil, salt and pepper and wrap between 2 sheets of parchment paper. Place in oven and bake for 6 minutes or until cooked through. Remove parchment paper, drizzle top of each with lemon juice then brush with cilantro pistou.

Cilantro pistou – purée cilantro, pine nuts and olive oil in blender until smooth. Season to taste with salt and pepper.

Artichoke barigoule – assemble sachet by wrapping first 4 ingredients in cheesecloth and tying together with kitchen twine. In medium pot combine stock, lemon juice, olive oil and sachet. Peel off outer leaves of artichokes. Peel skin at base of each plus stems. Cut off top of each artichoke where leaves start, but leave hearts intact. Add artichokes to pot and bring to simmer. Simmer for 10-12 minutes or until tender. Remove artichokes and scoop out hearts. Cut into ¼ inch dice. Transfer to container and add enough cooking liquid to cover them. Simmer remaining cooking liquid until reduced to 475ml.

The sauce – in a small saucepan, bring stock to boil. Add tapioca pearls and simmer until cooked and translucent, about 20 minutes. Strain and reserve the pearls. Purée artichoke cooking liquid with mustard; slowly stream in olive oil to emulsify. Mixture should coat back of spoon. Remove from blender and add tapioca pearls. Keep warm. When ready to serve, stir in cilantro.

Lemon arancini – bring chicken broth to a simmer in a large pot over a medium-high heat and hold at a slow, steady simmer. Meanwhile, in large sauté pan melt butter over medium heat. Add onion and cook, stirring just until translucent, about 5 minutes. Add rice, season with salt and pepper and cook, stirring, for about a further 5 minutes. Add 450ml of simmering stock. Cook, stirring often, until rice absorbs most of the liquid. Add another 450ml of hot stock; cook and stir as before. Continue cooking, stirring regularly and adding stock 450ml at a time until you have added a maximum of 2.7 litres. Taste rice for correct texture. Usually rice will need another 350-450ml of stock and a few more minutes to cook until firm but cooked through. Stir in cheeses, lemon juice and zest. Taste and season with salt and pepper. Pour rice onto parchment-lined 22.5x22.5cm baking sheet. Spread evenly and chill in refrigerator. When cooled, remove from baking sheet and slice into 2.5cm cubes. Coat each in cornstarch. Fill large pot ⅓ of the way with vegetable oil and heat to 177°C. Fry squares until golden brown. Transfer to paper towel-lined plate and sprinkle with salt.

Finishing and presentation – heat 6 12inch round dinner plates. In a small pan, heat fava beans and artichokes barigoule with 3tbsp of sauce; check seasoning. Spoon 2tbsp of artichoke-fava bean mixture onto bottom of each plate. Top with glazed piece of bass. Decorate top of each piece of fish with 4 squares of lemon arancini. Shave raw artichokes into medium bowl and toss with cilantro and chickpea tendrils in small amount of lemon juice and olive oil. Arrange salad on top of fish. Pour remaining sauce around fish and serve immediately. ■

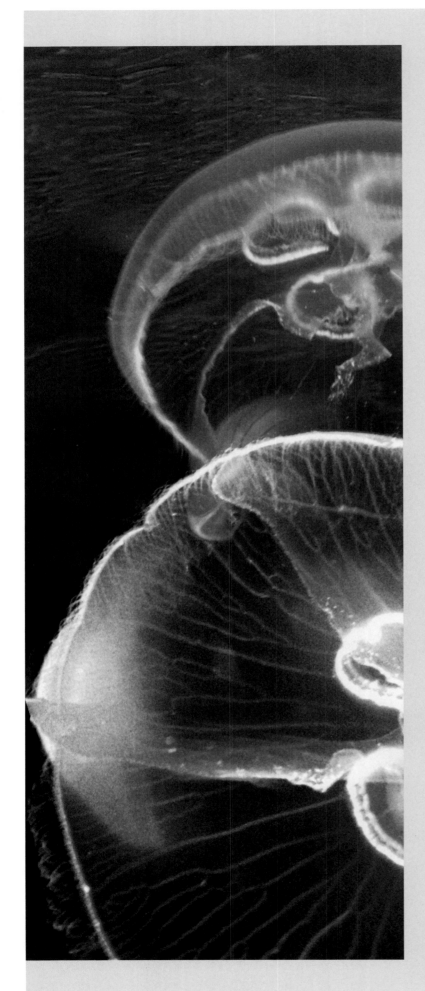

Bycatch

Bycatch is a term used for fish or other species caught unintentionally while intending to catch other fish. It is a very serious problem and the numbers are truly frightening:

- Over 300,000 small whales, dolphins, and porpoises die from entanglement in fishing nets each year, making bycatch the single largest cause of mortality for small cetaceans and pushing several species to the verge of extinction.

- Over 250,000 endangered loggerhead turtles and critically endangered leatherback turtles are caught annually on longlines set for tuna, swordfish, and other fish, with thousands more killed in shrimp trawls.

- 26 species of seabird, including 23 albatross species, are threatened with extinction because of longlining, which kills more than 300,000 seabirds each year.

- 89% of hammerhead sharks and 80% of thresher and white sharks have disappeared from the Northeast Atlantic Ocean in the last 18 years, largely due to bycatch.

- Shrimp trawlers catch as many as 35 million juvenile red snappers each year in the Gulf of Mexico, enough to have an impact on the population.

- Billions of corals, sponges, starfish, and other invertebrates are caught as bycatch every year.

Yet simple, proven methods already exist to reduce and even eliminate bycatch.

8

Al Brown
NEW ZEALAND

drop-out

At the leading edge of
New Zealand's food culture

Chef, TV presenter, writer and restaurant owner – Al Brown is one of the best known faces of the New Zealand food culture.

Chef Brown also has a passion for the outdoors, especially fishing and hunting, developed early in life through regular hunting trips with his family. His career path has taken him to North America, Europe and New Zealand where he received New Zealand's highest honour – Cuisine Magazine's 'Restaurant of the Year 2009', for his celebrated restaurant and bar, Logan Brown.

Along with his business partner Steve Logan, they have established a great 'foodie heaven' for residents of Wellington and further afield. Their aim has been to provide an eco-friendly restaurant, where every care is taken to only use the simplest fresh food, cooked to perfection; they pride themselves on complete awareness of where the fish is caught, or what goes into the ground where vegetables are grown. They work hard in this way to ensure that they have a positive effect on the environment, and this they have certainly achieved.

2009 also saw the launch of his new cookery book – Go Fish – which focuses on his love of fishing and seafood. ■

Al Brown

wild New Zealand black foot abalone

with crispy pork belly and ginger lime syrup

INGREDIENTS: (serves 6)

- 2.25kg pork belly
- 2tbsp flaked sea salt
- 750ml chicken stock
- 2 whole star anise
- 6 cloves
- 1 cinnamon stick
- 1-2 red chilli peppers (seeds to be removed optional)
- 30g ginger root (thinly sliced)

For the ginger and lime syrup:
- 45ml soy sauce
- 100ml rice wine vinegar
- 50ml white wine vinegar
- 2tbsp lime juice
- 120g rock sugar (smashed)
- 8g fresh ginger (julienne)
- 1-2 fresh chillis (sliced into thin rounds)

For the abalone:
- 6 black foot abalone

Assembly:
- Canola oil
- Pork belly
- 6 black foot abalone (room temperature)
- Ginger and lime syrup
- 75g each of cilantro leaves, chervil leaves, chive batons
- 2 whole limes

PREPARATION:

Pork belly – preheat oven to 120°C. For the pork belly, score the skin of the pork with a sharp knife, (a Stanley knife is perfect), then rub in the salt. Next place the pork into a suitably sized, high-sided roasting dish. Add the stock along with the star anise, cloves, cinnamon, fresh chilli and ginger to the pan. Cover with tin foil and place roasting dish on the stove top for 5 or so minutes until the stock is boiling, then place in the oven and bake for 1½ hours. The meat should be tender and moist. Now remove the foil and place the roasting pan under the grill to crackle the skin. Once the skin is crisp, remove and cool to room temperature, then chill. When the pork belly is set, take a sharp knife and trim the edges, then slice into 0.75cm slices. Refrigerate until required.

Ginger and lime syrup – place all the ingredients into a small non-reactive saucepan. Place on low heat and reduce by a third, to a slightly syrupy consistency. Remove, cool and store in the refrigerator.

The abalone – place the abalone on a clean towel. Take a meat mallet or rolling pin and lightly pound the abalone until the shellfish relaxes, and has the same thickness throughout. Refrigerate until required.

Finishing and presentation – pre-heat the oven to 120°C. Place a sauté pan on a medium heat. Once hot add a little oil then cook the pork belly slices for a minute or 2 on either side until golden. Remove and repeat with the remaining slices, then keep warm in the preheated oven. Take a skillet or sauté pan and place on a medium-high heat. Cut the abalone into 1.25cm thick pieces. Season the abalone slices with sea salt and pepper. Add a little cooking oil to the pan, then sear the slices for about 30 seconds on each side. They should be golden brown on the outside and still opaque in the centre.

To serve – on hot plates, alternate 3 pieces of the abalone with a couple of the crispy pork belly. Drizzle over a liberal amount of the ginger and lime syrup, then sprinkle over the fresh herbs. Garnish with a wedge of lime and enjoy! ■

Drop-out

Drop-out occurs while the net is being brought in. The decaying remains of fish and other marine animals that have died on the net fall off and are lost to the ocean. This is a terrible waste because not only does the bycatch fall off, but the fish that the net was put out for falls as well. This makes drift netting a very non-productive way of fishing and a waste of time and money.

There is thus good reason to ban drift nets altogether – worldwide. However, until such laws are enforceable and more easily regulated in the open ocean, the 'walls of death' will prevail and the unnecessary, indiscriminate slaughter will continue.

9

Ignatius Chan

SINGAPORE

shark finning

Iggy goes pop!

Ignatius Chan is the founder of the renowned 'Iggy's'. He is one of Singapore's most accomplished and awarded sommeliers and restaurateurs, renowned and respected far and wide. Known to his friends as Iggy, he always wanted to open a small, intimate restaurant that served exceptional food made from the very best ingredients; Iggy's is the realisation of that dream. The restaurant opened its doors in September 2004 to immediate acclaim.

Iggy's is designed to provide a gastronomic dining experience, coupled with personal, yet unintrusive, service. The cuisine is uniquely Iggy's – it is a culmination of the best of Ignatius' travel and dining experiences, marrying flavours and textures of seasonal ingredients from Europe, Japan and Australia, prepared with European techniques. Its original location was at the Regent Hotel but in September 2010 it moved to the Hilton. Since 2006, it has also been included in the S. Pellegrino World's 50 Best Restaurants list; in 2009 it became the first restaurant in South East Asia to be in the top 50 best restaurants, entering at number 45. 2010 saw the rise to number 28.

So what makes this charismatic man so popular? The sheer commitment to the profession? Perhaps his work ethic gained during his time working in establishments such as Singapore's Mandarin Oriental, the Crillon in Paris, the Ritz in Madrid, and the Relais & Châteaux Royal Champagne in Reims? Whatever the reason, he truly deserves his position in Singapore's high society. And when his busy schedule of work and travel permits, Ignatius likes to spend time at home with his wife and their three cats. ■

Ignatius Chan

little neck clams

with edible flowers and a sago and dashi sauce

INGREDIENTS: (serves 4)

- 24 New Zealand little neck clams
- 2 litres salted water
- 1 stalk lemongrass
- 5 garlic cloves
- 20g peeled ginger
- 6 datterini tomatoes (cut into quarters)
- 100g Buratta mozzarella cheese
- 8g tarragon
- 3ml lemon juice

For the edible flowers and herb garnish:
- 5g kaffir lime leaves (finely julienne)
- 5g tarragon
- 10g micro basil
- 5g micro parsley
- 30 petals of edible flowers

For the marinated rice:
- 250g Thai fragrance rice
- 1 zucchini
- 50ml grapeseed oil
- 100ml ponzu (citrus based juice)
- 100ml mirin (rice wine)
- 380ml water

For the sago and dashi sauce:
- 90g sago pearls
- 50g kombu (edible kelp)
- 1 sudachi (small round citrus fruit)
- 30ml bonito stock (please refer to preparation)
- Tsuyu (strong mixture of dashi and sweetened soy sauce)
- Salt to taste

PREPARATION:

Bonito stock – boil 250ml water to 80°C. Add in 10g of bonito flakes and 50g of kombu, cover with plastic film and infuse for 20 minutes. Strain the liquid and season with tsuyu and salt to taste. Keep the finished bonito stock in refrigerated storage.

Marinated rice – place 250g of Thai fragrance rice in pot and wash with water. Add 380ml of water and cook for 15 minutes in an oven at 165°C. When the rice is cooked, remove from oven and leave to cool. Take approximately 30g of cooked rice and mix with 50ml of grapeseed oil, 100ml of ponzu and 100ml of mirin to marinate the rice.

Sago and dashi sauce – boil 1 litre of water and 15g of sago pearls. Sago should be ready when it gets to a translucent state. Strain, leave to cool and place in the refrigerator. Add the sago pearls to 30ml of bonito stock with thin slices of sudachi. Stir well so that citrus, saltiness and umami flavours are balanced.

Little neck clam preparation – bring the water to a boil with the lemongrass, garlic and ginger for 2 minutes, add in the clams and continue boiling for 3 minutes, refresh in icewater, remove the clam meat and reserve.

Finishing and presentation – arrange 40g of the marinated rice mixture evenly over a sushi bamboo mat and roll it like sushi rice. Heat up a pan with 1 tablespoon of oil and a tablespoon of butter. Lightly sauté the clams in the pan with chopped tarragon, lemon juice, salt and pepper to emulsify the butter sauce and the clams. Arrange the datterini tomatoes in a row, followed by another line of the micro salad on the plate. Place the rolled rice beside the micro salad in three straight rows. Spoon the Burrata scattered over the rice and season with sea salt. Garnish with a few petals of edible flowers and micro herbs on the rolled rice. Finish plating the dish by spooning some sago and dashi sauce next to the marinated rice roll. ∎

We wanted to create a dish representing a scene of the ocean, beach and shells. The sago pearls are like the rolling waves, the rolled rice represents the beach and the little neck clams are like the shells on the beach.

Shark finning

Sharks have long been feared and thought of as the ocean's indiscriminate killing machines but they are highly specialised 'cleaners' in the marine ecosystem. They face, however, a considerable threat themselves and one of the most controversial fishing issues is shark finning – the process of cutting a fin off a shark to meet demand for shark fin soup, considered a delicacy in some Asian cultures, and traditional medicines.

Shark finning is done at sea and any shark is taken – regardless of age, size, or species. Furthermore, shark meat is not considered valuable and fishermen don't want to take up space by transporting whole bodies so the rest of the shark's carcass is cast into the ocean, sometimes still alive. When it re-enters the ocean, the shark is incapable of swimming upright, and dies. Never mind the cruelty involved, this is also a wasteful, damaging and unsustainable practice. Shark specialists estimate that more than 100 million sharks are killed for their fins annually and that lack of selection depletes shark populations faster than their reproductive abilities can cope. Sharks are top predators in the ocean, and play an important role in the ocean food web. They keep prey populations in check, so overfishing of sharks threatens the stability of the ocean ecosystem.

Shark finning violates the United Nations Food and Agriculture Organization's Code of Conduct for Responsible Fisheries and its Convention on the Trade of Endangered Species of Flora and Fauna (CITES) lists the whale shark, basking shark, and great white shark as species that could become threatened if trade is not controlled.

10

Robert Clark

CANADA

whaling

Robert was born in Montreal, Canada. He developed a keen interest in food at a very young age, he loved to forage alongside the fertile, salmon-abundant York River near his family home. He loved to cook the produce he found in the river which he believes gave him an appreciation for fresh fish.

Having undertaken formal culinary training in Ontario, after graduating in 1982, Robert's determination to learn from the best placed him in some of Toronto's finest kitchens including the legendary Three Small Rooms at the Windsor Arms Hotel. He also worked with some of Canada's foremost chefs, from whom he was constantly learning.

1990 saw him take a sabbatical in South East Asia and Australia, with his wife, Maureen Seay. They spent 18 months travelling, exploring the region's diverse gastronomic cultures. They eventually arrived in Vancouver, with new ideas, Robert had at last found his niche!

When Harry Kambolis decided the time was ripe to open a seafood restaurant, he recruited Robert to join his team, he was promoted to Executive Chef within the year. Since then, Clark's leadership at C Restaurant kitchen has been key to the restaurant's success, becoming one of Vancouver's prime destinations. It has subsequently won numerous awards for its distinctive cuisine and wine lists.

Clark recognises delicate balance of quality, diversity, sustainability and market demand that surrounds the seafood industry. He is a firm believer that, as a chef and a trendsetter in food, he not only has to be responsible about the food choices, also he can inspire change in the industry he has devoted his life to. He continues to dedicate huge efforts in seeking ingredients best in quality and sustainability. He also regularly contributes his time, to act as a culinary ambassador, helping promote British Columbia as a burgeoning seafood and agri-food producing region.

As a founding restaurateur in the Vancouver Aquarium's Ocean Wise Programme, Robert has deconstructed seafood supply lines, dealing directly with fishermen; this ensures a product that is of the highest quality, whilst respecting environmental sensitivities. ◼

A guardian of the oceans

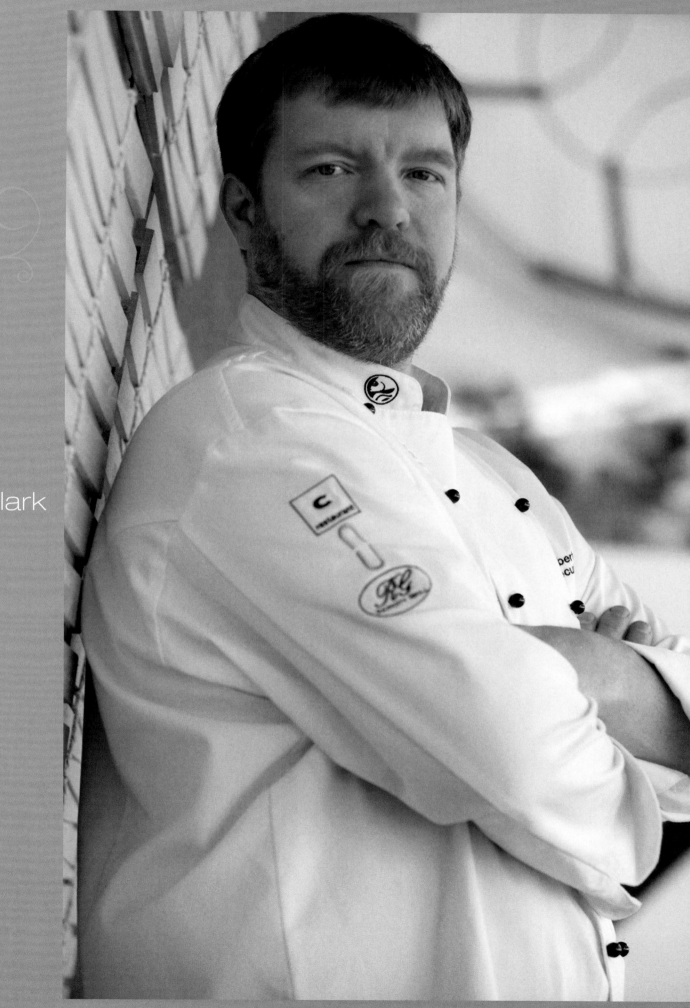

Robert Clark

seared albacore tuna salad

chilled summer vegetables, lemon herb dressing

PREPARATION:

For the tuna:
- 4 portions about 120g each
- 1tbsp chopped fresh tarragon
- 1tbsp chopped fresh parsley
- 1tbsp chopped fresh thyme
- Salt and pepper

Tuna – season the tuna portions and sprinkle with the freshly chopped herbs. Quickly sear on all sides leaving the tuna ultra-rare.

For the salad:
- 225g green beans, blanched
- 225g yellow beans, blanched
- 225g fingerling potatoes, cooked
- 60g radishes
- 60g cherry tomatoes, cut in half
- 225g watercress
- 225g asparagus, blanched

The salad – dress the vegetables with the appropriate amount of dressing.

Lemon herb dressing – purée all the dressing ingredients in a blender until smooth, refrigerate for up to a week or until needed.

Finishing and presentation – divide the tossed vegetables onto four plates. Slice the tuna and place attractively on top. Garnish the plate with the eggs and lemon wedges. Sprinkle sea salt on the exposed flesh of the tuna and serve. ■

For the lemon herb dressing:
- 125ml lemon juice
- 250ml extra virgin olive oil
- 2 medium shallots
- 2tsp of Dijon mustard
- 1tsp honey
- 2tbsp fresh basil
- 2tbsp fresh thyme
- 1tsp dried oregano
- Salt and pepper to taste

For the garnish:
- 4 whole hard boiled eggs, cut in half
- 4 lemon wedges

Whaling

Of all the issues that touch the plight of the oceans whaling is arguably the most emotional with barely a week going by without whalers and activists clashing, often with dangerous consequences. To indigenous peoples, like the Canadian Inuit, whale meat means the family doesn't starve and its oil means fuel, light – life itself in fact. To many, at the other end of the opinion scale, the statistics say it all. Despite a global moratorium, proclaimed by the International Whaling Commission (IWC), being in force since 1986, these creatures are still killed in large numbers; blue whales of the Antarctic, for example, are at less than 1% of their original abundance, despite 40 years of complete protection. Facing an even more acute problem, the West Pacific grey whale population hovers on the edge of extinction with just over 100 remaining.

Factors such as pollution and ship strikes threaten all whale species and industrial fishing depletes their food supply while simultaneously putting them at risk of entanglement in fishing gear. Nonetheless, the finger of suspicion in this sorry state of affairs points firmly to unscrupulous whaling activities and practices by countries such as Japan, who claim to kill in the name of scientific research, and Norway and Iceland, who reject the IWC line. This may be unfair, research can not be entirely sure. Whatever the cause in decline, expectations for the recovery of populations have been based on the assumption that their place in the oceans is as secure as it was a hundred years ago. Sadly, this assumption is no longer valid and that is why commercial and research whaling in all forms should be stopped.

11

Bart de Pooter

BELGIUM

an environmental **catastrophe** waiting to happen

The little community of Reet, just south of Antwerp, and its inhabitants are very fortunate, because this is where you will find Marie-Claire and Bart de Pooter's restaurant, Pastorale. This former presbytery has been converted into a restaurant of the highest gastronomic stands, and is one of Belgium's hidden jewels. It is a truly beautiful property with a warm contemporary design where every minute detail has been exacted.

Chef de Pooter's cooking is a melee of flavours and emotions which go straight to the heart, whilst simultaneously demonstrating culinary Flemish heritage just as it should be. He has one clear objective, and that is to offer the most unambiguous dish possible, demonstrating the quality of the produce and a dedication to exceptional tastes and flavours.

In contrast to global trends such as fast food, fusion or molecular cooking, Pastorale accentuates its rich Burgundian culinary tradition and creates a present day translation. Both technical and modern, this is cooking in constant evolution, where you will witness a natural harmony between a locale, a chef and his cuisine. Bart plays with sour and faint bitter accents using an intense sense of taste as the base of his dishes. They have an incredible richness and surprising structures, giving his light meals a playful tension that leaves a permanent impression.

Apart from being a linguist, this generous and affable chef also has a passion for art. He believes that the dishes on the plate should blend in with the space where they are eaten. This led him to commission the restaurant artist Arne Quinze to create a series of wooden sculptures and videos for 'My Home, My House and My Stilthouse.' In this newly renovated restaurant you will see that whilst the wood sculptures are not simply decorations, they are cleverly integrated in the rooms in a marvellous way to promote an atmosphere of calm. The 16 video screens located throughout the restaurant give the images an earthy, almost animal, aura. It is no surprise that Pastorale has 2 coveted Michelin-stars. ■

Welcome to My home, My house and My Stilthouse

Bart de Pooter

INGREDIENTS: (serves 6)

- 3 small lobsters
- 6tbsp olive oil
- 2tbsp lemon peel

For the quinoa salad:
- Quinoa (cooked)
- Shallots, finely chopped
- Ginger, grated
- Lobster meat (dice the meat from the legs and the excess of the tails)
- Green sancho pepper finely chopped
- Rice vinegar
- Lemon peel, finely grated

For the lobster cream:
- Yogurt
- Lobster sauce, reduced
- Lemon juice

For the popped amaranth:
- Amaranth

For the herbs / lettuce:
- Rocket
- Purslane
- Garden cress
- Turnip stems

For the turnip stem juice:
- 200g turnip stems, raw and peeled
- 20g mirin
- 170g crushed ice
- 20ml sushi vinegar
- Salt to taste

The quantities and ingredients are intended simply as a guideline for this dish.

lobster and quinoa salad

with popped amaranth

PREPARATION:

Lobster – boil the lobsters in court bouillon for 2 minutes. Break away the tail and carefully remove the meat from the shell, trim if needed. Do the same for the claws and use the meat for the quinoa salad and the shells for your lobster sauce. Sous-vide the lobster flesh from the tail in portion-size bags along with the olive oil and lemon peel. Place in water bath at 68°C for 4 minutes.

Quinoa salad – combine the lobster meat along with the shallots, ginger, green sancho pepper, rice vinegar and lemon peel, creating a lobster tartar. Present along with the cooked quinoa, simply taste and season accordingly.

Amaranth – cook the amaranth; dry it at 50°C and fry it in sunflower oil at 190°C. Leave to one side.

Turnip stem jus – mix all ingredients together in a high power mixer. Leave to one side.

Finishing and presentation – combine the lobster tartar with the quinoa and place on a serving plate and decorate the dish as shown, or to your own pleasure. ∎

An environmental catastrophe waiting to happen

Oceans have become the world's garbage dump – if you travel to the heart of the Pacific Ocean you'll find an island of garbage roughly twice the size of Texas. More recently scientists have discovered a comparable area of the North Atlantic Ocean where plastic debris accumulates. The 'plastic density' in these areas is 200,000 pieces of debris per square kilometre, with much of it small enough to be consumed by marine organisms. Seabirds in particular are adversely affected. When carbon dioxide is released into the atmosphere, the world's oceans absorb much of it. The water, in response, warms and acidifies, destroying habitats like wetlands and coral reefs. Oil spills, sewage and chemical leakages and agriculture run-offs collectively, too, are ceaselessly adding to the mire and reaping untold damage on a marine environment struggling to absorb the effluent of man.

12

Sven Elverfeld

GERMANY

dead
zones

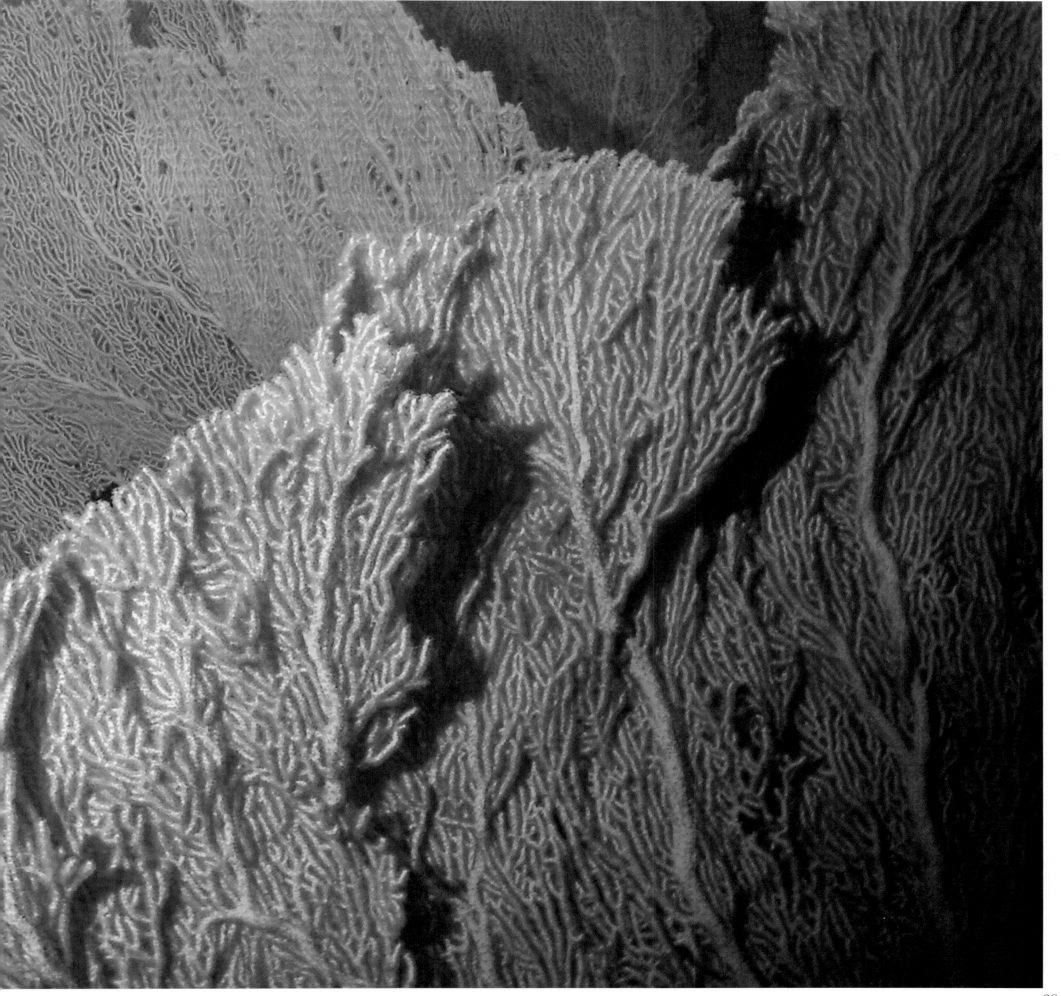

A man with a love for detail

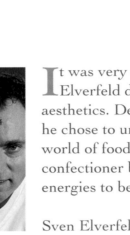

It was very early on in his career that Sven Elverfeld discovered his creative flair and love of aesthetics. Despite being an accomplished drummer, he chose to undertake an apprenticeship within the world of food and trained as a pastry chef and confectioner before completely dedicating his energies to becoming a chef.

Sven Elverfeld clearly belongs in the elite ranks of chefs in Germany. In 2009 he achieved his third Michelin-star for his restaurant Aqua and in 2010 he was elevated to the position of number 34 in the world by the accredited San Pellegrino Awards team who recognised his trend-setting German cuisine. The Aqua interior is very relaxing like a small oasis in the very technical and modern surroundings of this busy city.

Chef Elverfeld is a very modest and down-to-earth gentleman who has immersed himself in the deconstruction and reinterpretation of classic dishes from Germany and Europe resulting in a restaurant not to be missed! ■

Sven Elverfeld

poached Sylt Royal oysters

with artichoke cream and parsley

INGREDIENTS: (serves 4)

- 4 large Sylt Royal oysters

For the oyster foam:
- 70ml oyster juices
- 10ml champagne
- 20ml sparkling water
- A dash of lime juice
- Sugar, salt
- 10g Pro Espuma (Sosa)
- CO_2 capsule

For the artichoke purée:
- 2 small artichokes
- 1 shallot
- ½ clove of garlic
- 1tbsp olive oil
- 10ml white wine
- 10ml white port wine
- 200ml chicken stock
- 1 sprig of thyme
- Sugar, salt, white balsamic vinegar
- 1tbsp roasted, finely chopped pine nuts

For the parsley stock:
- 30g washed parsley
- 1 pinch vitamin C
- 4 ice cubes
- 10ml water
- Sugar, salt, pepper

For the parsley dust:
- A bunch of freshly picked and washed parsley

PREPARATION:

Oysters – shuck the oysters, retain the oyster juices and pass them through a sieve. Cut the cleaned oysters in half and place them in their juices. The oyster juices will be used for the espuma (foam) at a later stage. Poach the oysters in a light stock shortly before serving.

Oyster foam – peel the beans and throw away the skin. Cook with a little bicarbonate of soda in order to keep the colour. Rinse well. Place in the blender and make into a smooth purée. Keep to one side.

Artichoke purée – clean the artichokes and chop them finely. Cut the shallot into strips and sauté gently in olive oil with the garlic clove and the artichokes. De-glaze with white wine and white port wine. Add a touch of salt and pepper and then the thyme. Pour in the chicken stock and reduce the liquid until it is almost evaporated. Remove the thyme and the garlic. Purée the soft artichokes in a blender and season with white balsamic, salt, and pepper. Stir in the pine nuts before plating.

Parsley stock – blend all the ingredients together, strain and season.

Parsley dust – pluck the parsley leaves, wash them and spin them dry. Distribute them evenly on a plate with a paper kitchen towel. Dry in a microwave oven at full power turning once. Finally, push the parsley through a fine-meshed metal strainer. Store the resulting powder in a cool place in an air-tight container.

Finishing and presentation – place the artichoke purée in the middle of the small bowls and then place the poached oyster halves on top. Using a spoon, drizzle the parsley stock around the artichoke purée. Drizzle a few drops of lemon oil on top of the parsley stock. Spray the oyster espuma (foam) on the oysters and sprinkle with parsley. ∎

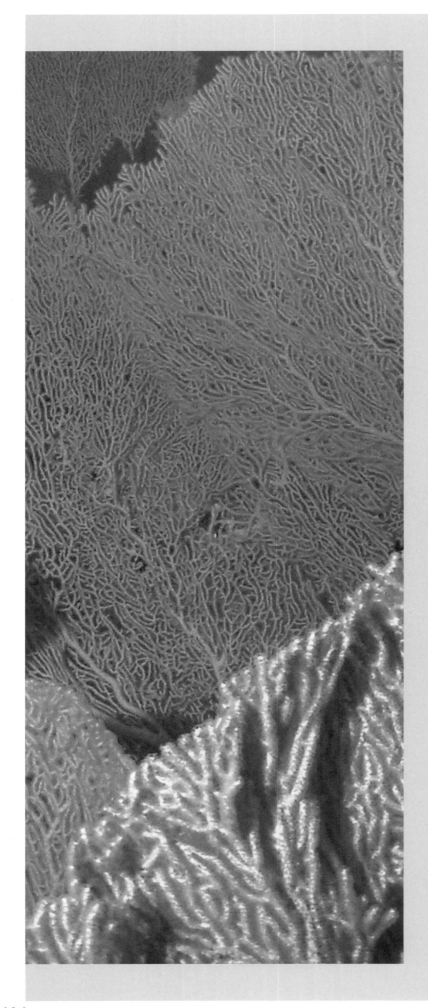

Dead zones

In a scenario replicated the world over, dead zones – areas of bottom waters too oxygen depleted to support most ocean life – are spreading. Fertilizer run off, the main culprit, and fossil-fuel use lead to massive areas in the ocean with scant or no oxygen (hypoxia), killing large swaths of sea life and causing hundreds of millions of dollars in damage. This fertilizer run off, instead of contributing to more corn or wheat, feeds massive algae blooms in the coastal oceans. This algae, in turn, dies and sinks to the bottom where it is consumed by microbes, which consume oxygen in the process. More algae means more oxygen-burning, and thereby less oxygen in the water resulting in a massive flight by those fish, crustaceans and other ocean-dwellers able to relocate as well as the mass death of immobile creatures, such as clams or other bottom-dwellers. And that's when the microbes that thrive in oxygen-free environments take over, forming vast bacterial mats that produce hydrogen sulphide, a toxic gas. The primary culprit in marine environments is nitrogen and the biggest contributor of nitrogen to marine systems is agriculture.

13

Andrew Fairlie

SCOTLAND

Andrew's appetite for cooking started at a young age when, aged just 15, he began a classical four year apprenticeship in his home town of Perth. At 20, he became the first recipient of the prestigious Roux Scholarship – a record that stands to this day. This was to change the course of his life, as it was to lead to an unprecedented honour for a British chef – to work in the kitchen of the French master, Michel Guérard. Guérard's approach was an inspiration to Andrew, and he still adheres to his mentor's ethos of 'simple food, brilliantly done'.

After working with Guérard, Andrew spent 14 months training at the world-renowned Hôtel de Crillon in Paris. Finally, after more than two years in France, he returned to his native Scotland to spend two seasons aboard the luxurious five-star Royal Scotsman. He then moved on to London, taking up a position with the Ritz Hotel as Senior Sous-Chef. Ultimately though, France beckoned once again and Andrew joined the opening team of the Euro Disney Group.

In 1995 he returned to Scotland where he became the Executive Head Chef at Glasgow's One Devonshire Gardens. He received not only acceptance into the esteemed Académie Culinaire de France, but also his first Michelin-star which he held until his departure in 2001. This was a very important period in the life of Andrew as he opened the eponymous restaurant within the heart of the legendary Gleneagles Hotel and Resort. Within six months of opening, it was awarded a Michelin-star and a stream of awards followed, along with the honour of being named by the US publication 'Hotels' as one of the top ten hotel restaurants in the world – it was the only British restaurant included. The pinnacle of Andrew's career to date came in 2006 when the restaurant was awarded its second Michelin-star.

2010 has resulted in Andrew signing an unprecedented 10 year lease to stay at the restaurant. He personally has self-funded and built a 'state of the art' bespoke gas-free kitchen. He has also chosen not to ignore technology but to embrace it, and as the great chef says "Molecular gastronomy, which originated at El Bulli, has had a huge effect on our world – it has stood the whole profession on its head!" In typical fashion, Andrew has used it to develop his menus even more. ■

The highlander – there can be only one

Andrew Fairlie

steamed fillet of Ghia halibut

clams and sea vegetables

INGREDIENTS: (serves 6)

- 6 x 60g filleted and skinned Ghia halibut
- 700g razor clams
- 120ml dashi
- 500g surf clams
- 100ml dry white wine

For the sea vegetables:
- 30g spiral wrack**
- 30g channel wrack**
- 30g samphire
- 30g sea lettuce
- 15g sea purslane

For the seaweed jelly:
- 230g water
- 230g seaweed
- 2.3g agar*
- Pinch of salt

*   *Agar see p14.*
** *Spiral wrack and channel wrack are species of seaweed, brown algae*

PREPARATION:

Seaweed jelly – bring the water to a boil and pour onto the seaweed. Leave to cool then strain the water into a saucepan. Add the salt and agar to the seaweed 'stock'. Whisk to a boil and simmer for 1 minute. Pour the hot liquid onto a clean, flat, shallow stainless steel tray (530mm x 325mm). Allow to cool and set completely. Using a very sharp knife cut the seaweed jelly to size so that it will fit neatly on top of each fish portion.

The razor clams – put the razor clams and dashi into a suitable vacuum pack bag and seal tightly. Cook the clams in a water bath at 60°C for 4½ minutes. Remove the bag of cooked clams from the water bath and allow to cool in the fridge. When the clams are completely cold, slice the white firm body part of the clam into 2mm rondelles. Chill until needed.

The surf clams – heat a heavy bottomed cocotte that has a tight-fitting lid. Gently tip the surf clams into the cocotte, quickly followed by the wine. Fit the lid tightly and cook them for 1 minute. Shake the pan to gently toss the clams and cook for a further minute. Tip the cooked opened clams and the winey juices into a colander. When they are still hot carefully pick the clams out of their shells and chill until needed.

Finishing and presentation – cut a disk of silicone paper to fit neatly into the bamboo steamer. Place the clam stock in the bottom compartment of the steamer. Sprinkle half of the sea vegetables and half of the cooked clams onto the silicone paper. Put the fish on top of the shellfish and vegetables and then sprinkle the remaining shellfish and vegetables onto the fish. Put the lid tightly onto the steamer and cook for 3 minutes. Using a pallet knife carefully remove the fish and place in the centre of warmed serving plates. Neatly place the steamed clams and sea vegetables around the fish. Top the fish with the jelly and spoon a little of the cooking juice around the vegetables. Serve at once. ■

Acidification

The National Oceanic and Atmospheric Administration (NOAA) of America estimates that the oceans have absorbed up to 50% of the carbon dioxide released from human activities. Whilst this uptake by the oceans benefits society by moderating the rate of climate change it also causes unprecedented changes to ocean chemistry. Within seawater there has been an increase in hydrogen ion (acidity) of about 30% since the start of the industrial age and although ocean acidification is an emerging field of research a growing number of studies have demonstrated adverse impacts on marine organisms:

- The rate at which reef-building corals produce their skeletons decreases.

- The ability of marine algae and free-swimming zooplankton to maintain protective shells is reduced.

- The survival of larval marine species, including commercial fish and shellfish, is reduced.

Peter Gilmore

AUSTRALIA

persistent organic pollutants

Inspired by nature

Peter Gilmore is arguably the best chef in Australia today. He was born and bred in Sydney, and at 19 years of age he left Australia to gain oversees experience, working in country house hotels in the UK. Three years later he returned, and spent the next ten years working in smaller establishments, including a spell as Head Chef of the De Beers restaurant at Whale Beach; it was here that he began to develop his own unique style of exploring the texture of food and its harmony of flavour. He would source food producers and learn to love the land, so much so that he is still a passionate gardener himself.

Now aged 42, he has been the Executive Chef at Quay restaurant since August 2001. Here, his original creative cuisine has seen the restaurant receive eight consecutive 'Three Chef's Hats' awards, together with a multitude of others including 'Restaurant of the Year' four times by the Sydney Morning Herald Good Food Guide. Quay is also ranked 27th in the S. Pellegrino World's 50 Best Restaurants 2010, and has been named 'Best Restaurant in Australia'.

Peter continues to refine his food, bringing new and exciting dining experiences to the table, with picture perfect dishes that celebrate nature's beauty. He is a chef in his prime, whose combination of extraordinary talent and rate humility has won him not just the highest accolades in the food world, but the respect and admiration of his peers. ■

Peter Gilmore

sashimi of Hiramasa kingfish

raw Chinese artichokes, pickled kohlrabi,
horseradish, smoked eel and egg white pearls

INGREDIENTS: (serves 8)

- 1kg Hiramasa kingfish fillet, skin removed,
  cut into 3mm slices, 6 per portion 7cm long
- 200ml white soy
- 1 x 500g octopus
- 32 Chinese artichokes
- 8 sticks white celery
- 20g freshly grated horseradish
- 200ml crème fraîche
- 200g piece daikon radish
- 2 kohlrabi
- 200ml good quality apple vinegar
- 50g castor sugar
- 32 small Nasturtium leaves
- 300ml ginger and spring onion infused grapeseed oil
- 50g smoked eel
- 500ml chicken stock
- 100g tapioca pearls
- Fine sea salt

For the smoked eel and egg white pearls:
- 70g smoked eel meat,boneless, skinless
- 200ml milk
- 70g white fleshed fish (cod or snapper)
- 60g mashed potato
- 60g softened unsalted butter
- ½ lemon, juiced
- 40ml extra virgin olive oil
- 30g crème fraîche
- 100ml strained egg white
- 500ml grapeseed oil
- Sea salt
- Nasturtium leaves for garnish

PREPARATION:

Smoked eel brandade – bring milk to boil, remove from heat, add smoked eel. Allow the eel to marinate in warm milk for 10 minutes. Strain, steam white fish until it flakes. Mix the eel with flaked white fish. Using a fork, mash the fish and eel together with half the softened butter. Drizzle half the olive oil and lemon juice onto the fish. Mix with fork. Mix in mashed potato. Add remaining butter, olive oil, mix well. Season to taste with sea salt. Allow mixture to cool, then fold in crème fraîche. Place in refrigerator for 1 hour. Take the mixture, roll out 8 balls, the size of a marble. You may have some additional mixture left over.

Egg white pearls – heat grapeseed oil to 70°C. Using an eye dropper, drop the strained egg white in the oil, drop by drop, in rapid succession. After you have about 30 droplets stop, gently stir around. They need 1 minute in the oil to fully set. Carefully sieve out the egg white pearls using a fine sieve, onto a flat metal tray. Repeat several times making sure you maintain the same oil temperature until you have sufficient amount of egg white pearls to coat the 8 marble-sized balls.

Shaping the brandades – line 8 demitasse cups with 12 x 12cm squares of cling film. Place a teaspoonful of egg white pearls in middle, spread them out. Place a ball of brandade in the middle, carefully lift the corners of the plastic together. The aim is to coat brandade balls in the pearls using the cling film. When you have 8 covered balls leave in refrigerator until required.

Microplane the fresh horseradish, fold into the crème fraîche, season. Slice daikon radish into 1mm slices. Cut the slices into 20mm discs. Blanch in boiling water for 2 seconds, refresh in iced water then dry. Place 1kg rice onto a flat tray. Spread rice to a depth of 3cm. Take a small square of cling film 7 x 7cm and place square onto rice. Use your finger to create an impression in the centre of the square to a depth of 2cm. Place 5 daikon discs in an overlapping circle on the cling film. Press the discs down in the centre. Using a piping bag, add a small dot of the horseradish cream in the centre of the discs. Unwrap the eel brandade pearls and carefully place each pearl in the centre of the daikon discs. Place the tray in the refrigerator for flowers to set.

Vegetables – wash the Chinese artichokes, cut celery sticks into julienne, lightly salt the celery, allow to marinate for 1 hour. Rinse celery. Divide celery into 16 small bunches, twist each bunch into a spiral and put aside. Dissolve the sugar in the apple vinegar, peel kohlrabi, slice to a thickness of 1mm, cut slices into 2cm wide strips. Place in the vinegar, marinate for 1 hour.

The octopus – remove the tentacles, rinse with some coarse sea salt, scrub under running water. Once rinsed, remove the suckers with a sharp knife horizontally, cut into small lengths. Reserve 1 more tablespoon of ginger grapeseed oil, heat the remaining oil in a small saucepan to 70°C. Poach the sliced octopus for approximately 1 minute. Remove the octopus and drain.

Kingfish fillet – remove skin and most of the bloodline from the fillet. Cut the kingfish into 3mm thick slices across the fillet. You will need 6 slices per portion. Your slices will be approx. 7cm long.

Finishing and presentation – briefly marinate kingfish slices in white soy (10 seconds). Drain the slices and brush on the remaining ginger grapeseed oil. Squeeze out all vinegar from pickled kohlrabi. In the bottom of each serving bowl place 2tsp of horseradish crème fraîche. Place a small bundle of pickled kohlrabi on top of crème fraîche and then 3 slices of the marinated sashimi kingfish. Next place another 2tsp of horseradish crème fraîche on the kingfish, another small bundle of pickled kohlrabi and then the other 3 slices of marinated kingfish. Garnish with Chinese artichokes, celery twists, smoked eel tapioca and then place a smoked eel and egg white flower in the centre of the dish. Finally garnish with Nasturtium leaves and serve. ■

Persistent organic pollutants

Persistent organic pollutants (POPs) are organic compounds that are resistant to environmental degradation through either chemical, biological, and photolytic processes. Because of this, they have been observed to persist in the environment, to be capable of long-range transport, accumulate in human and animal tissue, magnify through food chains, and to have potential significant impacts on human health and the environment. One study (Cullon et al 2009), published in the journal Environmental Toxicology and Chemistry, revealed that chinook salmon off the coast of British Columbia are highly polluted with persistent organic pollutants (POPs), and that these toxins are passed on to their predators, the resident killer whales. Contaminant levels varied widely by location but as an example polychlorinated biphenyls (PCBs), a toxin known to affect reproductive and immune function in mammals, was just one of the many toxins uncovered in this study.

Many POPs are currently, or were in the past, used as pesticides. Others are used in industrial processes and in the production of a range of goods such as solvents, polyvinyl chloride, and pharmaceuticals. Though there are a few natural sources of POPs, most POPs are created by humans in industrial processes, either intentionally or as byproducts.

15

Hans Haas
GERMANY

coral reefs

Hans Haas was born in 1957 in Wildschönau, in the Austrian Tirol. He started his career as an apprentice in Austria, where he worked until 1980; he then moved to France to join Chef Paul Haeberlin at the Restaurant Auberge de L'Ill as Chef de Partie, before moving on to work with Eckart Witzigmann at the restaurant Aubergine in Munich, Germany. From these two renowned chefs he learned a great deal, developing his passion for artistry in the kitchen, his professional ethics and perhaps even more importantly, his staying power!

In 1987 Hans took his first Chef de Cuisine position at the restaurant Brückenkeller in Frankfurt. From here he joined restaurant Tantris, leading the team there and achieving much notoriety en route to gaining two-Michelin-stars. Additionally, he was awarded third place at the prestigious Bocuse d'Or in Lyon. In 2005 Gault Millau awarded him 'Chef of the Year', and many other awards and accolades were to follow.

As for his food, Hans' dishes mirror his temperament – refreshingly natural, product driven and creative. Chef Haas has written four cookery books and has opened his own cookery school; whatever spare time he has left is spent sculpting and skiing. ■

Simply for enjoyment

Hans Haas

sardines in a 'tempura sepia ink batter'

in a herbal curry cream

INGREDIENTS: (serves 4)

For the herbal curry sour cream
- ½ tsp curry powder
- ½ tsp grounded Curcuma (turmeric)
- 300g sour cream
- Salt
- Lime juice
- 50g spring onions, some cut in longish rings, the rest cut very fine
- 1 bunch finely cut chives
- 1 bunch finely cut parsley
- ½ bunch finely cut dill
- ½ bunch finely cut coriander

For the sardines:
- 4 sponged sardines
- 4 tsp cold eggplant sauce
- Salt
- Flour for coating
- Corn oil for deep-frying

For the charcoal batter:
- 150g tempura flour mix
- 250ml ice water (or 250g crushed ice)
- 50g corn oil
- 50ml sepia ink
- 1 pinch of salt

Additionally:
- 1 tbsp sour cream
- 1 tsp lobster coral

PREPARATION:

Herbal curry sour cream – boil curry powder with Curcuma, with 2-3 tablespoons of water and stir in the sour cream. Taste with salt and lime juice. Add herbs, except the spring onions, and place it in the fridge.

Take off the head of the sardines and cut along the side to keep both body parts connected at the tail. Disembowel the fishes, carefully remove the bones, wash and dry on a kitchen towel. Fill each fish with 1 teaspoon of eggplant sauce and fold the fish up.

Charcoal batter – mix the tempura flour mix with ice water. Stir in oil and sepia ink, add some salt. The dough needs to be icy cold. Salt the sardines and cover with flour. Dredge through the dough and fry crispy in 180°C hot oil. Place the sardines for a short moment on kitchen paper.

Finishing and presentation – put the herbal curry sour cream onto the plates and place 1 sardine on top. Garnish with cut spring onions. Mix the sour cream with the lobster coral and draw a line around the fish. ■

Coral reefs

Coral reefs are part of the foundation of the ocean food chain. Nearly half the fish the world eats make their homes around them. Hundreds of millions of people worldwide – by some estimates, 1 billion across Asia alone – depend on them for their food and their livelihoods. If the reefs vanished, experts say, hunger, poverty and political instability could ensue.

Numerous studies predict coral reefs are headed for extinction worldwide, largely because of global warming, pollution and coastal development, but also because of damage from bottom-dragging fishing boats, errant ship navigation and the international trade in jewellery and souvenirs made of coral. At least 19% of the world's coral reefs are already gone, including some 50% of those in the Caribbean. An additional 15% could be dead within 20 years, according to the National Oceanic and Atmospheric Administration.

Exotic and colourful, coral reefs aren't lifeless rocks; they are made up of living creatures that excrete a hard calcium carbonate exoskeleton. Once the animals die, the rocky structures erode, depriving fish of vital spawning and feeding grounds. If reefs were to disappear, commonly consumed species of grouper and snapper, for example, could become just memories. Oysters, clams and other creatures that are vital to many people's diets would also suffer. Quite simply, commercial fisheries would fail miserably at meeting demand for seafood, fish will become a luxury good and the economic repercussions could be enormous.

16

Thomas Keller
U S A

Chef Thomas Keller is as renowned for his culinary skills as he is for his ability to establish world class restaurants and businesses. He is a man of exceptionally high personal standards and values.

He began his culinary career at a young age, working in the Palm Beach restaurant managed by his mother. He moved to France in 1983, where he worked in several Michelin-starred restaurants including Guy Savoy and Taillevent. He opened his first restaurant, Rakel, in New York in 1986, before moving westward to California to work as the Executive Chef at the Checkers Hotel in Los Angeles.

In 1994, Chef Keller opened the French Laundry in Yountville, which quickly became a destination restaurant on the culinary world map. His French bistro Bouchon opened in 1998 and the Bouchon Bakery followed 5 years later. He now has eight restaurants and two bakeries in the United States. In 2005 he was awarded the three-star rating in the inaugural Michelin Guide for Per Se, and in 2006 he was awarded three stars for the French Laundry.

This truly incredible chef has a wonderful philosophy: "In the end, a great meal is not about the food and the wine. A great meal is an emotional experience. We try hard to make it an extraordinary one by creating a beautiful place, one filled with staff who care about it as they do about their home, and care for you as the most important guest in it. Our chefs are obsessive about the culinary details and fundamental techniques that are the foundation of an exciting culinary imagination, and a kitchen that delivers the very best products of the earth to the table. No detail or element can be less important or more important than another, because a great meal is not one that fills you up. A great meal is a kind of journey that returns you to sources of pleasure you may have forgotten, and takes you to places you haven't been before." This philosophy is shared by all of his team.

It is difficult within this space to capture the amazing achievements of this great master, which include America's 'Best Chef' awards from the James Beard Foundation and 'Chef of the Year' by the Culinary Institute of America. He is the only American born chef to hold multiple three-star ratings by the Michelin Guide. He is also a publisher, olive oil producer and is involved in the world of film and television. ∎

Simply a genius

Thomas Keller

Photography Deborah Jones

133

INGREDIENTS: (serves 6)

For the abalone:
- 6 small farm-raised red abalone (approx. 8.75cm)
- 2 litres water
- 50ml distilled white vinegar

For the brine:
- 875ml water
- 125ml lemon juice (approx. 3 lemons)
- Zest from 3 lemons
- 50g salt
- 50g sugar
- 1 litre canola oil

For the Haas avocado purée:
- 1 Haas avocado
- 30g crème fraîche
- 15ml lime juice
- Salt

For the basil gastrique:
- 65g water
- 65g sugar
- 25ml lime juice
- 10g basil leaves coarsely chopped
- 1½ tbsp of basil seed

For the lime salt:
- 2tbsp Maldon salt
- Zest of 1 lime grated on microplane*

For the cucumber and melon:
- 1 firm ripe Galia melon
- 2 English cucumbers
- 1 Japanese cucumber (if unavailable just use a smaller English cucumber)
- Cucumber blossoms (optional)
- 1tbsp peppery, grassy olive oil such as one from Tuscany

For the garnish:
- Small basil leaves picked and refreshed in ice water

*   *Microplane – a fine hand grater.*
**   *Mandoline – kitchen slice.*
*** *Chinois see p14.*

salad of Monterey Bay abalone

Galia melon, cucumber, Haas avocado and basil

PREPARATION:

Abalone – (one day ahead) – remove abalone from shell by sliding a large spoon underneath flesh (going in from flat side of the shell). Carefully trim off all organs from abalone. Under warm running water, gently use a scouring pad to remove black surface surrounding the edges. Soak abalone in 2 litres of warm water with vinegar for about a half hour or until muscle relaxes and feels somewhat tender. Remove abalone from water and place on a tea towel. Place another towel on top and gently pound with a smooth mallet until abalone is tender and flimsy. Score the brown foot side of abalone 60mm deep at 60mm intervals creating a cross hatch pattern. Combine 875ml water with the lemon juice, sugar, salt and zest and place in a container. Heat the canola oil in a 3 litre pot to 182°C. Fry each abalone individually until they 'pop' into a porcupine shape (about 30 seconds). Remove abalone from oil and place in the lemon solution. Allow to chill in solution overnight in a refrigerator.

Haas avocado purée – split avocados in half and remove seed. Scoop pulp from skin and remove any blemishes. Coarsely chop avocado and place in blender with lime juice. Blend until creamy then add crème fraîche and blend until just incorporated. Pass through chinois*** and season with salt. Place avocado purée in a squeeze bottle or piping bag. Chill.

Basil gastrique – soak basil seeds in cold water until hydrated, reserve. Combine water and sugar in small saucepot and bring to boil. Cook until large bubbles form and the syrup thickens. Remove from heat and allow to cool for a minute or so. Stir in lime juice then add basil and let steep for about 5 minutes. Strain the syrup then strain the basil seeds and combine with the syrup. Allow to chill.

Lime salt – grate the lime zest and combine with the Maldon salt. Store chilled in a sealed container until ready to use.

Cucumber and melon – peel English cucumber and remove seeds from melon. If you have access to a vacuum sealer, vacuum cucumber and melon in separate bags to compress them until they have a translucent appearance. Dice melon in large, medium and small dice, 3 to 4 pieces of each is sufficient for each abalone. Set melon aside to chill. Dice the cucumber into very small dice, a tbsp per abalone is plenty. Rinse the Japanese cucumber, pat dry. Slice cucumber into very thin rings on a mandoline**. Toss the slices with kosher salt and allow to wilt and release excess liquid. Pour off excess liquid then place the sliced cucumber in iced water to refresh. The cucumber slices should be both wilted but crisp. Drain off ice water and dry the cucumbers as much as possible without damaging them. Reserve chilled.

Finishing and presentation – dress the diced melon and cucumber with olive oil, season with lime salt. Remove abalone from brine, pat dry. Dress abalone with olive oil and a little lime salt. Mound and scatter the cucumber and melon dice somewhat randomly on a chilled plate. Prop the abalone up on one of the larger mounds. Squirt dots of avocado purée around abalone and garnish. Also drizzle small dots of basil gastrique. Dress shaved Japanese cucumber with a little olive oil and arrange small piles and folds around plate. Garnish with basil leaves and cucumber blossoms. ■

Coastal development

With global urbanisation and the move of populations to megacities, often close to the coast, the associated development and construction projects are in danger of adversely affecting the biological diversity of marine ecosystem. Where supervision is lax or where economic imperatives supersede that of any other then land reclamation, a process in which natural and man-made materials are added to coastal areas and waterfronts in an attempt to make them more solid, is increasingly claiming offshore wetland. These new surfaces have a tendency to change the ocean functions and affect the direction of water currents so that in some instances fish cannot swim to certain places to lay their eggs and thus will eventually disappear.

Undeniably our favourite place is the sea and according to the United Nations, 60% of the world's population – more people than inhabited the entire planet in 1960 – now live within 60km of the coast. As coastlines around the world are steadily turned into new housing, holiday homes and tourist developments, this intense human presence is inevitably taking a huge toll on marine ecosystems and species.

Yoshihiro Narisawa

JAPAN

At harmony with nature; guided by earth, water, forest and fire

Yoshihiro Narisawa was born in April 1969 in Japan. At the age of 19 he moved to France where he worked under culinary maestros such as Joël Robuchon, Frédy Girardet and Paul Bocuse. Some eight years later he returned to his native Japan to open La Napoule restaurant in Odawara, just outside Tokyo and by the sea. This attracted gourmets from all over Japan. In 2003 he moved to Tokyo's famed Minami Aoyama district to open his now renowned Les Créations de Narisawa.

Chef Narisawa respects the Japanese traditional calendar of seasons, and translates this into modern cooking. He understands nature as a chef through his themes of 'earth, water, forest and fire.' His cuisine is neither French nor Japanese, but simply Narisawa style, drawing lots of attention from around the world.

Natural recurrence and gastronomy is also present in Narisawa cuisine. His philosophy is that one should not only be eating a meal, but they should absorb life itself. In chef Narisawa's own words "follow mother nature to maintain your healthy body and mind." He believes that through the experience of eating, his creations may inspire people to open their eyes to nature.

This wonderful restaurant has previously been voted the best in Asia and also ranks as number 24 in the S. Pellegrino World's 50 Best Restaurants for 2010. ■

Yoshihiro Narisawa

INGREDIENTS: (serves 4)

- 4 250g live, unshelled black abalone
- 7cms rectangle of kombu
- 120ml sake
- Sherry vinegar
- Black pepper, salt and water for the sauce

For the wild edible plants:
- 200g Sansai (wild edible plants such as:- akamizu, aomizu, hamabofu, hosotake, shidoke, aido, aokogomi, akakogomi, zenmai, warabi, taranome, koshiabura, gyojyaninniku, urui)

For the luxury essence:
- 2kg of duck
- 2 litres water
- ½ carrot
- ½ leek
- ½ celery stalk
- ½ clove of garlic
- 200g jamón ibérico (without fat)
- 15g purified agar* (kanten)

Finishing:
- Olive oil and clarified butter (nutty brown)

* *Agar see p14.*

'mountain and the sea'

abalone from the sea and edible wild greens
from the mountains

PREPARATION:

Abalone – rinse four 250g live, unshelled black abalone, then place in a cooking tray with the shells down. Lay 1 7cm rectangle of kombu over each abalone and drizzle with 120ml of sake. Cook for 5 minutes at 100°C in a steam oven. Remove just the livers and cool them down by placing in iced water. Cook the abalone again in the oven for 1 hour. Press livers through a sieve, then place in a pot with sherry vinegar, black pepper, salt and water to make the sauce.

Wild edible plants – separately boil 200g Sansai, wild edible plants (from the listed selection), in salted water until cooked, then plunge into ice water to retain the colour.

'Luxury essence' – place the 2kg duck, 2 litres water, the carrot, leek, celery stalk and the garlic in a stainless steel tray. All ingredients should be cool, before cooking for 3 hours at 95°C in a steam oven. Remove from the oven and let stand until residual heat has dissipated. Strain through paper and simmer down until there is 1 litre of liquid. Place the duck essence and 200g jamón ibérico (without fat) in a tray. The ingredients should be cool before cooking again in the steam oven at 95°C for 3 further hours. Remove from the oven and strain through paper once the residual heat has dissipated. Heat the essence and add 15g purified agar (kanten). Pour into a stainless steel tray and solidify. Cut into 9cm squares.

Finishing and presentation – sauté the abalone cooked to softness in a frying pan with olive oil and butter. Heat Sansai with steam and season with salt and nut brown clarified butter. Arrange the abalone on a plate, drizzle with warmed abalone liver sauce, cover with Sansai and top with the clear 'luxury essence' jelly. ■

'Mountain and the sea'

This dish is composed of abalone from the sea and Sansai (edible wild greens) from the mountains. It is taken from the mountain and ocean scenery in the early days of spring. The vegetation sighs silently underfoot while water from the melted snow flows down the mountain, dampening the earth and soothing the roots of the trees. Before long this water meets seawater, and in that place, high quality abalone is nurtured. This is a dish showing gratitude from mother nature.

This abalone that tastes sweeter as you chew, along with the bitter flavour of wild Sansai sprouts, is served covered by a transparent veil of jamón ibérico. Once it is cut with a knife, the wintery scene portrayed on the plate is over and spring arrives.

Offshore drilling

Brought starkly into focus by the Gulf of Mexico oil spill in the Spring of 2010, human demand is driving ever more adventurous and technically challenging extraction of oil and gas resources offshore. Inevitably, in pushing the boundaries of technology, accidents happen and as anyone who's ever dressed a salad in vinaigrette will testify, oil and water just don't mix. That's especially true of crude oil and seawater that supports lifeforms from fish to birds to plankton to mammals. Such activity therefore deserves increased scrutiny but 'peak oil' has been reached and the world still strives inexorably for more; the likelihood of stemming the tide of offshore drilling is thus problematical unless attitudes and behaviour are changed.

No oil spill is entirely benign. Even a relatively minor spill, depending on the timing and location, can cause significant harm to individual organisms and entire populations. Regarding aquatic spills, marine mammals, birds, bottom-dwelling and intertidal species, and organisms in early developmental stages – eggs or larvae – are especially vulnerable. Whilst the effects of oil spills can vary greatly, oil spills can cause impacts over a range of time scales, decades in some cases. The challenge facing responsible policy-makers now is how to meet the planet's booming energy demand without threatening our natural world.

18

Enrique Olvera
MEXICO

noise pollution

One of the new wave, revolutionising Mexico's cuisine

Olvera was born in Mexico City but moved to New York to undertake his professional studies at the Culinary Institute of America, where he graduated with honours. Since then he has achieved many accolades and awards. Food and Wine, one of the world's most recognised gastronomy publications, chose Olvera as one of its most promising figures in world cuisine; he was named 'Chef of the Decade' by Chilango Magazine, whilst GQ Mexico named him as one of the 2009's most talented Mexicans.

In 2000, Enrique returned to Mexico City to open his own restaurant, Pujol. It is widely recognised as one of Mexico's most interesting and creative gastronomic destinations. At just 33, he is a key figure in the Mexican culinary avant-garde that in recent years has raised the nation's cuisine to the highest and most demanding of international standards.

As an inventor, he likes to play with his food. He is not satisfied to just give his clients point-perfect reproductions of traditional dishes, he dissects and deconstructs them and then puts them under a metaphorical microscope, rethinking and remodelling Mexican cuisine.

In 2010 Pujol celebrates its tenth year, and to coincide with this Enrique has just published his first book 'Uno', a compilation of texts by various authors, as well as dozens of recipes, comic strips, photos and stories. His book leaves the reader in no doubt as to how Pujol represents Mexico's food revolution. ■

Enrique Olvera

Photography Fiamma Piacentini

trout with pumpkin seed and árbol mojo

potato escabeche and kale juice

INGREDIENTS: (serves 6)

For the trout:
- 6 portions of trout fillet
- 3tbsp arbequina olive oil
- Sea salt

For the kale juice:
- 500g kale leaves (stems removed)
- 60g butter
- Sea salt

For the fried kale:
- 6 kale leaves
- Grapeseed oil

For the potato escabeche:
- 50ml sugar cane vinegar
- 10g Mexican oregano
- 2 jalapenos
- 1 potato
- 3 pimienta gorda (allspice)

For the mojo:
- 100ml arbequina
- 20g garlic oil
- 2 dried árbol chile
- 20ml fresh lime juice

PREPARATION:

Trout – fillet the trout and place in a vacuum-sealed bag and put in a water bath at 60°C for 8 minutes.

Kale juice – place the kale leaves in a juicer in order to produce approximately 300ml of juice. Transfer to a small pan and warm and whisk in whole butter. Season with salt. Leave to one side.

Fried kale – fry kale leaves in grapeseed oil, place over paper towels to drain excess fat.

Potatoes – cut potatoes into 1mm thick slices, blanch in boiling water for 3 minutes. Strain, pat dry. Mix the oregano, vinegar, pepper, sugar, water and pimienta gorda together. Place the liquid in a bag, add potatoes, put them in a vacuum bag, seal and rest for 5 hours.

Mojo – heat olive oil in a sauté pan, add garlic and chile. Cook gently until caramelized, deglaze with lime juice. Season with salt.

Finishing and presentation – arrange the prepared fillet on the serving plates, top with the sliced potatoes and drizzle with the mojo mixture. Carefully place the fried kale around the fish and then spoon around the kale juice. ◼

Noise pollution

As if the previously articulated problems are not enough, fish are being threatened by rising levels of man-made noise pollution. Scientists have reviewed the worldwide impact on fish species of noises made by oil and gas rigs, ships, boats and sonar and assess that increasing noise levels severely affect the distribution of fish, and their ability to reproduce, communicate and avoid predators. The level and distribution of underwater noise is growing at a global scale but receives very little attention, largely because the phenomenon is concealed by the fact that underwater sounds are difficult to hear by people living in air. Cetaceans, i.e. whales and dolphins, are particularly affected. They become disoriented, cannot find mates or food and behave differently; a growing number of cases of stranding of whales and dolphins are believed to be linked to sound pollution. Some draw the analogy of a cocktail party effect: you have to speak louder and louder until no-one can hear each other anymore.

To make matters worse, researchers have recently realized that man-made carbon dioxide not only warms and acidifies the ocean – it also affects acoustical properties of seawater, making it more transparent to low-frequency sound. The impacts of these changes in ocean acoustics is not yet fully understood but because of decreasing sound absorption, underwater sound could travel farther, and this could lead to growing noise levels at distance, similar to the effect when the bass on a music system is turned up.

Noisy seas

- 80% of global freight transport takes place by motorised shipping.

- The global shipping fleet comprises around 1.2 million vessels.

- Underwater sounds are produced by navies, fisheries, the oil and gas industry and scientists.

- Fish-finding echo sounders have been used by fishing boats since the 1950s.

Ashley Palmer-Watts

UNITED KINGDOM

A shining light

Originally from Dorset, Ashley Palmer-Watts' love of food began with his country upbringing, which introduced him to the exceptional seasonal produce of the British Isles. An after school washing up job in a local restaurant at 13 ignited a passion for cooking which resulted in a career spanning almost 20 years. After leaving school he started work at Le Petit Canard in Dorset, where he learnt the fundamental disciplines of the kitchen whilst spending most of his free time visiting producers and suppliers.

Ashley joined Heston Blumenthal at The Fat Duck in Bray in 1999, when it had just received its first Michelin-star. Within two years, he was promoted to Sous-Chef, and he became Head Chef in 2003. Since 2008, he has been the Executive Head Chef for The Fat Duck Group. In November of 2010, Ashley will open 'Dinner by Heston Blumenthal' at the Mandarin Oriental hotel in Knightsbridge, London.

His creative eye for detail, coupled with a great enthusiasm for researching British ingredients, has enabled Ashley to create with Heston a unique menu of historically-inspired British dishes for the new restaurant. He continues to oversee development at The Fat Duck and the Hinds Head in Bray.

In addition to a very full life in the kitchen, Ashley loves spending time with his wife Emma and young son Max, and indulging in his passion for photography, fast cars and just the odd game of golf! ■

Ashley Palmer-Watts

Photography eddiejuddphotography.com

bergamot-cured mackerel

with garlic and anchovy sauce

INGREDIENTS: (serves 4)

For the mayonnaise:
- 36g egg yolks
- 20g Dijon mustard
- 180g arachide oil (peanut oil)
- 10g Chardonnay vinegar
- 2g salt
- 40g lemon juice

For the garlic & anchovy sauce:
- 75g garlic cloves, peeled and de-germed
- 4 x 300g semi-skimmed milk for blanching the garlic
- 200g semi-skimmed milk
- 8g panko breadcrumbs
- 50g anchovy fillets
- 42g olive oil
- 15g lemon juice
- Mayonnaise (from above)

To cure the mackerel:
- 25g sugar
- 75g salt
- 20g bergamot zest
- 10g lime zest
- 10g coriander seeds
- 2g black peppercorns
- 2 fresh mackerel

To serve:
- 6 grelot onions, peeled, blanched, cut in half (similar to small pearl onions)
- The peas from 8 fresh pea pods, blanched
- 16 Bull's Blood leaves
- 8 endive leaves, blanched for 5 seconds and cut in half
- 4 pea shoots
- 25g olive oil
- 25g bergamot juice

PREPARATION:

Mayonnaise – combine the egg and mustard together in a bowl. Gradually incorporate the oil, whisking continually to emulsify. Add the vinegar, salt and lemon juice and mix well. Refrigerate until required.

For the garlic & anchovy sauce – cover the garlic with 300g milk and add a dash of cold water. Bring slowly to a simmer then drain and rinse the garlic under cold running water. Return the garlic to the pan and repeat this process 3 more times. In a pan, cover the garlic with the 200g of milk and bring to a simmer. Allow to cook until the garlic is very soft and the milk has reduced in volume. Remove from the heat and pour into a jug. Blitz using a hand blender until smooth, then add the breadcrumbs and anchovy fillets and blitz again until smooth. Whilst blitzing, slowly add the olive oil and lemon juice then pass through a fine sieve. Weigh the garlic and anchovy mix, add 30% of the total weight of mayonnaise and mix well. Refrigerate until required.

To cure the mackerel – place the sugar, salt, bergamot and lime zest, coriander seeds and peppercorns in a food processor and blitz until finely ground. Gut and fillet the mackerel. Run the tip of a sharp filleting knife down either side of the pin bones and bloodline in the centre of each fillet and gently remove this area by pulling it away with a pair of fish tweezers. Spread the bergamot cure onto a tray and place the fish fillets on it, flesh-side down. Cover with cling film and refrigerate for 2 hours. Rinse the fillets under cold running water to remove the cure then pat dry with kitchen paper.

Place a nonstick pan over the lowest possible heat. Wipe the bottom of the pan with a very thin layer of olive oil. Place fillets one at a time skin-side down in the pan and apply gentle pressure by hand to ensure that every part of the skin is in contact with the surface of the pan. Cook for approximately 10 seconds or just enough to soften the skin. Remove from the pan and place flesh-side down on a tray lined with greaseproof paper. When all the fillets have been cooked in this way, place the tray in the fridge to cool the skin down.

Finishing and presentation – when ready to serve cut each fillet into 4 pieces. Spread a tablespoon of garlic and anchovy sauce on each plate and place the mackerel pieces on top. Garnish with the onions, fresh peas, Bull's Blood leaves, endive and pea shoots. Whisk together the olive oil and bergamot juice and drizzle a little around the dish before serving. ∎

Ocean governance

The ocean is a unique, extraordinary and vital element of our planet, covering more than 70% of its surface. It sustains life on Earth by generating oxygen, absorbing carbon dioxide from the atmosphere, regulating climate and temperature and providing a substantial portion of the global population with food and livelihood. It provides medicine, energy, transport routes amongst many other services and has been a nexus for various cultures. National jurisdiction and sole use over resources extends to 200 nautical miles in the sea, leaving about 60% of the ocean as 'high seas' and deep seabed outside any one state's control. Yet, there is no comprehensive policy or management framework to govern the high seas, and the patchy laws that exist are largely based on 17th century principles of open access, ignoring many of the environmental principles that have been long applied for land and atmosphere and even for outer space.

Today's global maritime order is based on a delicate geo-political and judicial balance between two central but essentially competing ideas that have existed in a state of tension for some four hundred years:

The first is mare liberum – the concept that the seas cannot be made sovereign and hence are free for all to use, a sentiment that is still pervasive in our global cultural consciousness.

The second is mare clausum – the idea that the seas can be made sovereign to the limits of effective control by states.

That delicate balance was achieved through an unprecedented degree of international consultation in the closing decades of the 20th century that led to the United Nations Convention on the Law of the Sea, or UNCLOS. Governments are now the only entities that can take this collaboration another step forward to prevent the end of fish.

20

Daniel Patterson

U S A

ocean
policies

Super natural Northern California cuisine

Daniel Patterson differs from many other chefs in that he is self-taught. At the age of 25 he opened his first restaurant Babette's in Sonoma, California; that was 1994, and was followed some years later by the opening of Elisabeth Daniel in San Francisco. His work was truly loved by all, and awards such as 'Chef of the Year' and 'Best New Restaurant' were bestowed upon him. April 2006 saw the opening of Coi in San Francisco, where in 2008 it gained its two-Michelin-stars.

Daniel's cooking skills are extremely innovative and he is dedicated to finding the best ingredients in his area; he also respects the carbon food print, harvesting cultivated plants grown from heirloom seeds. He uses wild leaves, flowers, barks and roots, local fish, seaweed and coastal grasses, as well as pastured meat, poultry and eggs from small farmers. Additionally he brines, cures and smokes using traditional methods, and at the same time embracing modern cooking techniques. The dishes at Coi are animated by flavours and textures, some familiar and some strange! This is Northern Californian cuisine as it appears through the eyes of Chef Patterson.

Daniel has written for the New York Times, Food and Wine, London Financial Times and San Francisco Magazine. He is currently working on his second book. Daniel has also achieved recognition in the global arena, and has previously been invited to present at the Omnivore Festival in France and at Fusión in Madrid. ■

Daniel Patterson

Monterey Bay abalone grilled on the plancha

nettle-dandelion salsa verde, spicy breadcrumbs, wild fennel flowers

INGREDIENTS: (serves 4)

- 4 young abalone, thinly sliced and tossed with a tbsp of olive oil
- 1 lemon
- Fresh wild fennel flowers
- Nettle-dandelion salsa verde
- Spicy breadcrumbs

For the nettle-dandelion salsa verde
- 75g nettles, cooked quickly in salted water, rinsed, drained and finely chopped
- 50g dandelion greens, cooked quickly in salted water, rinsed, drained and finely chopped
- 12g shallot, minced
- 25g champagne vinegar
- 40g caper berries, finely diced
- 55g green olive oil
- 25g lemon juice
- Salt

For the spicy breadcrumbs
- 40g almonds, roasted and finely chopped
- 40g pain de mie, toasted and finely chopped
- Salt
- Dried and powdered ripe Padrón pepper

PREPARATION:

Monterey Bay abalone – spread the abalone on a plate and season with salt. Cook quickly on a lightly oiled very hot cast iron pan, stirring frequently, until just cooked, about 30 seconds. Remove to a small mixing bowl. Season the abalone to taste with lemon juice and salt. Spread a large spoonful of nettle-dandelion salsa verde in a bowl. Put the abalone on top. Zest a little lemon on the abalone and dust with spicy breadcrumbs. Snip a few wild fennel flowers on top.

Nettle-dandelion salsa verde – mix the shallots, vinegar and some salt in a bowl. Let stand for 20 minutes. Stir in all other ingredients. Season with salt, and add more oil, vinegar or lemon juice as necessary.

Spicy breadcrumbs – mix all ingredients and season.

Finishing and presentation – take all ingredients and arrange in an artful way on your chosen dish. ■

Ocean policies

In a growing awareness of the value of oceans, a number of countries, most recently the USA, have developed comprehensive ocean policies in order to protect, maintain, and restore the health and biological diversity of ocean, coastal, and lake ecosystems and resources. To some these initiatives represent a slow erosion of constitutional rights but it is precisely because the same individuals and organisations have treated the oceans irresponsibly that the need to establish more far reaching policies has unfolded.

The effectiveness of these policies rests fully with the ability to uphold the law and the capacity to act. One example of this is Canadian Forces aircraft and crews providing annual support, codenamed Operation Driftnet, to Fisheries and Oceans Canada (DFO) to help enforce national and international fishing regulations in the western Pacific. However, the level of commitment is by no means consistent amongst nations. Nonetheless, in forming a national ocean policy the critical role of oceans in providing and facilitating jobs, food, energy resources, ecological services, recreation and tourism opportunities, transportation, economy and trade is at least recognised.

Jacques & Laurent Pourcel

FRANCE

united nations
convention on the
law of the sea

171

When the 'Jardin des Sens' opened in 1988 Montpellier, France, twins Laurent and Jacques Pourcel were only 23... 20 years and three-Michelin-stars later, these French globetrotting chefs enjoy promoting their culinary skills all over the world, never failing to amaze with their know-how and ingenuity.

Laurent and Jacques may be twins but it is clear that the two brothers are very different. Although equally discreet and with the same modest look and attitude, Laurent is extremely reserved and rarely leaves the kitchen; meanwhile Jacques passes through every now and again, in between trips abroad to open a new restaurant or to brief an expatriate kitchen team who have been sent to another part of the world.

Prior to the opening of their famous restaurant the twins lived out their culinary passions separately. Laurent worked with Michel Bras and Alain Chapel, whereas Jacques worked with Michel Trama, Marc Meneau and Pierre Gagnaire. The result is two different career paths, two experiences and two separate culinary cultures, all acquired with the most emblematic leaders of French cooking.

French culinary 'brothers in arms'

The chefs have created an unpretentious and inconspicuous restaurant façade. Behind it all is a secret heaven: a Japanese-style garden and a stairway planted with lemon and olive trees and umbrella pines, as well as fragrant bouquets of lavender, rosemary, thyme and verbena... hence the name 'Jardin des Sens'!

Undoubtedly the colours, textures, fragrances combined in an atmosphere of calmness, enhance the experience of the culinary pleasures being created in a kitchen which is happy, innovative and fun. These true artists of sweet and sour, bittersweet and crunchy-tender dishes, look at cooking as a playground where the only rules are creativity, extravagance and harmony. Their cooking starts with the base product and plays on contrasts, and their aim is to have the guest understand what they have done and how they have created it. This is something that they achieve to a superlative level.

Their success has also pushed them to venture abroad, especially to Asia where the Pourcel brothers now have restaurants in Tokyo, Bangkok and Shanghai. ■

Jacques & Laurent Pourcel

oven baked sea bass

Provence's green asparagus with lemon
confit vinaigrette

INGREDIENTS: (serves 6)

- 1 sea bass about 1.5-2kg
- 24 green asparagus
- 3tsp of olive oil
- Juice of 1 lemon
- 3 shallots
- 1 peeled and diced tomato
- 6 confit tomatoes
- Chives
- Salt and pepper
- Szechuan pepper
- Fleur de Sel

For the beurre monté:
- Boiling water
- Chilled butter cut into cubes

For the lemon confit:
- 3 lemons
- 200g sugar

PREPARATION:

Sea bass – cut 120g pieces out of the de-boned fillet. Place them on a baking tray covered with foil and slightly oiled. Keep them in the fridge.

Asparagus – peel, wash and boil the asparagus in salted water. Once they are cooked, cool them down as quickly as possible in an iced water bath.

Lemon confit – cut thin slices of lemon. Place them in a pan with the sugar and add some water to cover the lemons. Cook on medium heat for 2 hours. Refrigerate them. You can dry some lemon slices on a baking tray in the oven at 60°C for the decoration of the dish.

When ready, chop about 10 pieces of the lemon confit and mix them with the lemon juice, olive oil, the chives, the shallots and the diced tomato. Add a bit of warm water.

Beurre monté – remove boiling water to one side, slowly whisk in cubes of the chilled butter until it emulsifies, keep at a temperature of about 88°C until ready to use.

Finishing and presentation – bake the sea bass fillets at 120°C for 12 minutes. Warm up the asparagus in a 'beurre monté' and season them. Plate the asparagus on the bottom of the serving dish or plate, cover them with the vinaigrette. Take off the skin of the fish, season it with Szechuan pepper and Fleur de Sel. Place the dried lemon on the side. You can also add some fresh thyme and some tomato confit to garnish the dish. ■

As 'brothers Pourcel' used to say the main ingredient is your imagination!

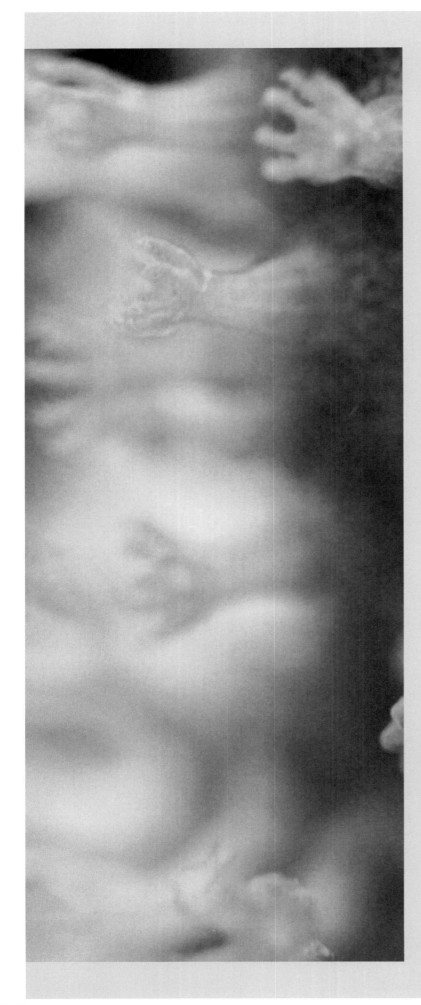

United Nations Convention on the Law of the Sea

UNCLOS is arguably the crowning legal achievement in global history, but what made it possible is the fact that the maritime powers and coastal states risked suffering equally from an unregulated, disputed and unstable maritime order. However, it's by no means assured that the remarkable consensus embodied in UNCLOS will withstand the tremendous changes and pressures on the maritime regime that we are currently witnessing. Beyond national jurisdiction, many human activities remain unregulated, ecosystem considerations are seldom taken into account and scientific information is often ignored. We stand at a critical time – the ocean governance system, no matter the complex legal challenges faced, must evolve and modern principles applied to improve high seas management to ensure sustainable development of the world's oceans. Technology can overcome past limitations of enforcing ocean regimes but the corporate political will to commit resources to this task must be more forthcoming.

Principles of High Seas Governance

Nature has its own set of rules and it is appropriate for policies to reflect these rather than the laws of economics that appear only to give diminishing returns. Herewith proposed principles for High Seas Governance put forward by the International Union for Conservation of Nature (IUCN):

- Conditional freedom of activity on the high seas

- Protection and preservation of the marine environment

- International cooperation

- Science-based approach to management

- Public availability of information

- Transparent and open decision making processes

- Precautionary approach

- Ecosystem approach

- Sustainable and equitable use

- Responsibility of States as stewards of the global marine environment

22

Paul Rogalski

CANADA

regional
seas
programme

Chef Paul Rogalski is renowned for his passion for home grown and sustainable cuisine. He is co-creator, along with Olivier Reynaud, of the acclaimed Rouge Restaurant in Calgary, Canada, ranked 60th in the world in the prestigious San Pellegrino World's Best Restaurants Awards 2010.

At a very young age and influenced by his grandparents, Paul discovered his passion for quality ingredients, cooking and business. He spent time with his grandmother, Katherine Rogalski, harvesting fresh produce from her garden to cook for dinner. He was taught the meaning of flavour through the incredible Ukrainian feasts for which she was famed. At the same time, his grandfather Jack Middleton introduced him to the world of butchery, through his renowned Bon Ton Meat Market; even today this is recognised as a landmark gourmet meat shop in Calgary.

Creativity, freshness and utilising seasonal and locally grown ingredients are the beliefs that Paul truly stands for. His passion for travel, photography and adventure can also be found influencing his cuisine, where he creates fun and playful food concepts. He is a delightful character, living life to the full, and yet is completely focussed when it comes to his culinary profession.

In 2009, Paul received special recognition for 'Leadership and Support of Organic and Sustainable Cuisine' from the Monterey Bay Aquarium, for his work as a Seafood Watch Ambassador. He is a member of the Slow Food of Canada and the Chaîne des Rôtisseurs. ■

A 'fun loving' kind of guy

Paul Rogalski

halibut tea

and vegetable 'lava lamp'

INGREDIENTS: (serves 6 as an appetiser)

For the vegetable bubbles:
- 235ml bell pepper juice, seasoned to taste
- 1tsp agar* powder
- 235ml cucumber juice
- 3.8 litres canola oil (chilled in a deep freeze to -15°C)

For the tea:
- 1.3kg raw halibut bones (rinsed under cold water)
- 28g unsalted butter
- 2 medium-sized onions
- 4 celery stalks (medium diced)
- 1 medium fennel bulb (medium diced)
- 1 leek white (cut lengthways, washed then medium diced)
- 28g ginger, finely chopped
- 1 lemongrass (cleaned and thinly sliced)
- 5g flat-leaf parsley (leaves and stems roughly chopped)
- 6 branches fresh thyme
- 22g black peppercorns
- 120ml dry white wine
- 2.4 litres very cold water
- 1tsp sea salt
- 4 large sprigs of fresh dill (cleaned and chopped)

Agar see p14.

PREPARATION:

Vegetable bubbles – make this in advance. Soften the agar in 3tbsp of the bell pepper juice. Meanwhile heat 8tbsp of the bell pepper juice to a simmer. Pour the agar mixture in the simmering bell pepper juice, dissolve completely and return to a simmer and immediately remove from heat. Add remaining room temperature bell pepper juice and stir until smooth. Using a large syringe, gather the mixture and slowly drip into the frozen canola oil allowing pearls to form. Continue until mixture is finished. Harvest the pearls with a wire mesh scoop and rinse with cold water. Refrigerate for future use. Re-freeze canola oil and repeat method with cucumber juice.

The tea – melt the butter in a heavy pan over a medium heat. Add vegetables, lemongrass, parsley, thyme, ginger and peppercorns. Cook until the vegetables become transparent stirring frequently to avoid browning. Place the halibut bones on top of the vegetables evenly. Add salt, wine and enough very cold water – just to cover the bones. Bring the stock to a simmer over a high heat. Reduce heat to low as soon as a soft simmer has been achieved. Be careful not to boil. With a soft touch, continually remove the foam and continue cooking for 30 minutes. Do not disturb the stock by stirring or shaking or the stock may become cloudy.

Carefully siphon or strain the stock through a very fine mesh strainer or cheesecloth into another stockpot or heatproof container, agitating the bones as little as possible. Season to taste. For the best aromatics, serve immediately. Alternatively, place strained stock in an ice bath until temperature reaches 4°C. Refrigerate for future use. Heat to 83°C when ready to use.

Finishing and presentation – organise glass serving dishes large enough to hold all of your portions, add the vegetable bubbles and the sprigs of dill. Carefully top with the warm halibut tea. Stir and pour into serving dishes in front of your guests. ■

Regional Seas Programme

Under the auspices of the United Nations Environment Programme (UNEP) the Regional Seas Programme is a long-standing initiative that aims to address the accelerating degradation of the world's oceans and coastal areas through sustainable management. It does this by engaging with and encouraging neighbouring countries to adopt comprehensive and specific actions to protect their shared marine environment. More than 140 countries participate in 18 regional seas programmes and in most cases action plans are underpinned with a strong legal framework in the form of regional conventions and protocols.

Nonetheless, whilst outwardly laudable and well-intentioned, about 60% of global ecosystems services and fish stocks remain in sharp decline. The weakness is widely acknowledged as inadequate governance and the associated lack of capacity to patrol the 'commons' to ensure compliance and inability to enforce the agreed rules and regulations. Hence, without proper policing the oceans continue to be plundered and resources misappropriated. Efforts to strengthen these mechanisms and the practical application of conventions must be given the highest priority.

23

Clare Smyth

UNITED KINGDOM

marine
protection
areas

Clare Smyth's steep rise to Head Chef at the three-Michelin-starred Restaurant Gordon Ramsay is not surprising, considering her exemplary credentials. Clare's devotion to her craft, her uncompromising standards and her meticulous work ethic are just some of the reasons why she remains the first and only female chef in the UK to run a restaurant with this accolade.

Clare's childhood on a farm in County Antrim, Northern Ireland, gave her a healthy respect for local produce and this interest in the provenance of ingredients is very much evident in her cooking today. Being a chef was more than a passing interest for Clare it was a vocation; and so, at the age of 16, she moved to England to learn the skills which would eventually make her a world class chef. On completing her studies, Clare further quenched her thirst for knowledge by working under many influential chefs around the world.

On her return to the UK Clare joined St. Enodoc Hotel in Cornwall, and by the age of 21 became Head Chef. But Clare's passion and dedication was still driving her forward, and in 2002 Clare joined Restaurant Gordon Ramsay, where Gordon detected Clare's natural flair and talent. She worked her way through the kitchen to become Senior Sous-Chef, then in 2005 Clare left. With her sights set on working with Alain Ducasse, she travelled to Monte Carlo and joined Le Louis XV.

In 2007 Clare returned to London and to Restaurant Gordon Ramsay, having further developed her culinary skills. With a wealth of experience under her belt she had the ideal attributes to take the reins of a restaurant, and in 2008 she became Head Chef of this renowned establishment.

Her dedication to excellence has ensured that Restaurant Gordon Ramsay is still the epitome of fine dining, and Clare has been an inspirational mentor for the many young chefs who look to follow in her footsteps. ■

A star is born

Clare Smyth

INGREDIENTS: (serves 6)

For the lobster:
- 6 native Scottish lobster (approx. 450g)
- 6 carrots, 6 sticks of celery, chopped into 3cm pieces
- 4 onions, chopped into 3cm pieces
- 4 leeks (white parts only), chopped into 3cm pieces
- 800ml white wine, 200ml white wine vinegar, 8 litres water

For the lobster butter:
- 2 lobster heads, 500g unsalted butter, diced

For the herb farfalle:
- 6g rocket leaves, 6g baby spinach leaves, 6g basil leaves
- 1tsp lemon juice
- 5 egg yolks
- 150g pasta flour
- 50ml chicken stock
- 20g butter
- Parmesan cheese, grated
- 1tbsp Barolo vinegar

For the acidulated cream:
- 50g double cream, 50g crème fraîche
- 1tsp lemon juice, salt to taste

For the lobster glaze:
- 2 lobster heads
- 1 carrot, 1 onion, 1 leek chopped into 3cm pieces
- 50ml vegetable oil
- 600ml chicken stock, 400ml veal stock
- 1tbsp tomato purée
- 50g butter, cubed and chilled

For the wild garlic flower and leaves:
- 1 egg
- 50ml milk
- 10g flour
- Wild garlic flowers, picked from garlic leaves used for garnish
- 40g wild garlic leaves, olive oil

For the asparagus:
- 12 spears of asparagus, 50ml chicken stock, butter

For the morels:
- 12 morel mushrooms, 50ml white wine, 100ml chicken stock, butter

butter poached Scottish lobster tail

with English asparagus, morels, wild garlic and herb farfalle

PREPARATION:

Lobster – place chopped vegetables in pot, add liquid ingredients, bring to a boil to make a bouillon. Break apart the lobster, separating the head, body and claws. Reserve heads. Poach lobster in bouillon, about 2 minutes, lift out, allow to cool slightly. Remove the meat, set aside.

Lobster butter – open lobster heads, discard the soft tissue. Chop remaining shells and legs into small pieces, place in a roasting pan. Cover with diced butter. Bake for 2 hours at 140°C. Let cool slightly, sieve, pouring off only clear clarified butter. Chill to set.

Farfalle – mash the rocket, spinach, basil and lemon juice with a mortar and pestle until a fine paste. Scoop the paste into bowl, whisk in yolks. On a smooth surface, pour the flour into a mound, making a well. Slowly pour in yolk mixture, mixing the flour gradually using your hands. Knead dough together until incorporated, lightly dusting the surface with more flour as needed. Work the dough until smooth, wrap with cling film, let rest for 30 minutes at room temperature. Roll the dough (0.5cm thick). Cut into 3cm fluted rounds. Pinch the pasta circles from top to bottom to create farfalle. Place on a tray and set aside.

The cream – whisk cream and crème fraîche together in a large saucepan over medium high heat. Let simmer, reduce by a quarter. Purée with hand blender. Season with lemon and salt.

Lobster glaze – start by preparing lobster heads as per lobster butter recipe. Roast the chopped heads, colour, add chopped vegetables. Stir in tomato purée, cook, about 1 minute. Add stocks, simmer ½ hour. Strain, reduce until thickened, 10-15 minutes, whisk in the cold butter.

Garlic flowers and leaves – pick white flowers off the leaves, set aside. In a small bowl, whisk together the flour, eggs and milk to make a beignet. Dip the flowers in the batter, deep fry until crispy golden. Place garlic leaves into a hot pan with some olive oil. Season with salt and cook until wilted.

Lobster butter – divide butter, four equal parts, place into separate vacuum pack bags. Add equal amounts of plain butter to each, one tail, one claw, and a pinch a salt. Seal, poach in a 63°C water bath for 15 minutes. Carve lobster, coat, finish with lobster glaze.

Asparagus – trim, place in a hot pan with olive oil. Tip in the chicken stock, cover, let steam for about 5 minutes until tender. Add a knob of butter to glaze. Season.

Morels – heat up a knob of butter until foamy. Add morels, sauté until soft, season with salt, pour in white wine, reduce. Deglaze pan with chicken stock, cook covered for 5 minutes.

The farfalle pasta – bring a pot of salted water to the boil. Cook farfalle until al dente. Drain, place in large saucepan. Toss with chicken stock, butter, Barolo vinegar and parmesan to taste.

Finishing and presentation – see photograph for best presentation. ■

Marine Protection Areas

The laudable concept of establishing Marine Protected Areas (MPA), an idea being pursued by Greenpeace and others, is encouraging countries to consider a 'big picture' approach to saving the seas and to recovering and then preserving life within them. Just 0.2% of the world's oceans are protected, compared with nearly 11% of the world's land mass. Therefore international agreements, such as the Convention on Biological Diversity (CBD), have set a looming deadline of 2012 to create a network of worldwide MPAs in national waters and on the high seas. Sadly, although most countries have agreed to these targets, few are on track to reach them.

Nonetheless, envisaged is a global network of high seas marine reserves, highly protected areas that are off limits to all extractive and destructive uses, including fishing. They are the most powerful tool available for the conservation of ocean wildlife and paradoxically may also benefit fisheries by promoting recovery and reproduction of exploited species. Such a network aims to protect places that are biologically rich, supporting outstanding concentrations of animals and plants. It would also seek to protect places that are particularly threatened or vulnerable to present or possible future human impacts, like fishing or seabed mining. The overarching goal is for a network that is representative of the full variety of life in the sea and to be truly effective the network must be large enough to sustain species and ecological processes in perpetuity.

The British government has recently created the world's largest marine reserve, designating a group of 55 islands in the middle of the Indian Ocean off-limits to industrial fishing and other extractive activities. The Chagos Islands are home to roughly half of the Indian Ocean's healthy coral reefs, along with several imperilled sea turtle species and 175,000 pairs of breeding seabirds. The new preserve covers 210,000 square miles – an area larger than California and more than twice the size of Britain – and will shelter at least 76 species classified as endangered by the International Union for Conservation of Nature.

24

Masa Takayama

U S A

maritime spacial planning

Masa Takayama grew up in Nikko, a small town north of Tokyo, where his parents had a fish shop and catering business. When he was not at school, he and his siblings spent their time loading fish into the display case before delivering their father's sashimi to customers by bicycle. Takayama began cooking in his early teens, and after graduating from high school he moved to Tokyo, where he was hired by the well-known sushi restaurant, Ginza Sushi-ko. He began working at the very bottom as a bathroom cleaner and dishwasher, and worked his way up to Sushi Chef. Eight years later, in 1980, Takayama moved to Los Angeles where he worked at a number of Japanese restaurants, eventually opening his own Ginza Sushi-ko.

Today, Chef Masayoshi Takayama can be found at New York's Time Warner Building. This tiny sushi temple seats just 10 at the sushi bar, and 26 guests in the main dimly lit dining room; the restaurant is replete with burbling water, brushed clay walls, and a retinue of sushi acolytes, their heads shaved like monks, working silently behind the bar. There are no menus at Masa; the chef simply adjusts his meals according to the availability of ingredients. The meals are an intricate and lavish cultural experience – part nourishment, part entertainment, and part ancient performance art. Chef Takayama not only creates the menu and prepares the food, he sometimes even serves it too!

As one well-known critic rhapsodised: "Masa engineers a discreet moment of pure elevation". It's no surprise that he has gained three-Michelin-stars, among other awards. In addition to his culinary genius, he is an enthusiastic potter and an avid marathon runner. ■

A temple to the gods of sushi

Masa Takayama

Photography Sophie Munro

kawahagi kutsuki

triggerfish with white truffle

INGREDIENTS: (serves 6)

For the cured triggerfish:
- 72g kawahagi, triggerfish, filleted
- 2 sheets kombu seaweed

For the salad combination:
- 10g white truffle julienne
- 12g fried maitake mushroom tips, julienne
- 6g kuchiko julienne*
- 4g shio kombu, julienne***
- 4g micro mizuna**

For the white truffle sauce:
- White truffle, finely grated
- White sesame oil
- Pinch of Himalayan salt as the seasoning

For the garnish:
- Yellow ginkgo leaves
- Gold flakes

*   *Kuchiko – dried sea cucumber ovaries.*
**   *Micro mizuna – Japanese salad greens, its saw toothed leaves resemble the leaf of a dandelion, but more tender and delicate with a mild mustard flavour.*
*** *Shio kombu – a leathery seaweed often cooked in soy sauce or seasoned water, then dried and cut into strips. Can be used in a dashi stock and is umami rich in flavour.*

PREPARATION:

Kawahagi triggerfish – lightly cure the triggerfish with sea salt for 15 minutes then press between 2 sheets of kombu seaweed. After this process thinly slice the kawahagi into julienne strips. Set aside.

White truffle sauce – combine the grated white truffle, sesame oil and sea salt into a paste and set aside.

Salad combination – toss all the ingredients lightly together in a large bowl.

Finishing and presentation – gently mix the triggerfish and the truffle sauce with the salad combination, ensuring that the julienne mixture is placed delicately in a decorative serving bowl. As per the photograph it should have height. Lightly shower with a sprinkling of ginkgo leaves and gold flakes.

Inspiration – "This dish came to me in the fall of 2000 when I moved from Los Angeles to New York. I was walking through Central Park and the wind was gently drifting over the leaves and almost naked branches of the trees; this was such a beautiful moment in time captured perfectly by nature. This moment, this feeling is what I wanted to capture and translate into my dish; this moment inspired me. The branches reminded me of finely julienned truffle fried maitake mushroom and kombu seaweed. The green leaves led me to mizuna and the yellow ginkgo leaves of course the gold flakes. Kawahagi is the perfect fish for this dish as this is its season, it is lightly cured and also julienned with a white truffle sauce drizzled over." ■

Maritime Spatial Planning

National interests in the ocean, coastlines and lakes support a growing number of significant and often competing uses and activities, including commercial, recreational, cultural, energy, scientific, conservation and homeland and national security activities. Combined, these activities profoundly influence and benefit coastal, regional, and national economies and cultures. However, human uses of the ocean, coasts and lakes are expanding at a rate that challenges the ability to plan and manage them under a more traditional sector-by-sector approach.

The concept, therefore, of Maritime Spatial Planning (MSP) offers a comprehensive, adaptive, integrated, ecosystem-based, and transparent spatial planning process, based on sound science, for analyzing current and anticipated uses of ocean, coastal areas and lakes. MSP identifies areas most suitable for various types or classes of activities in order to reduce conflicts among uses, reduce environmental impacts, facilitate compatible uses, and preserve critical ecosystem services to meet economic, environmental, security and social objectives. In practical terms, MSP provides a public policy process for society to better determine how the ocean, coasts and lakes are sustainably used and protected now and for future generations.

MSP is intended to improve ecosystem health and services by planning human uses in concert with the conservation of important ecological areas, such as areas of high productivity and biodiversity; areas and key species that are critical to ecosystem function and resiliency; areas of spawning, breeding, and feeding; areas of rare or functionally vulnerable marine resources; and migratory corridors.

In the Netherlands a 'preferred sand mining area' has been identified within its territorial sea. This use allocation through marine spatial planning will allow sand extraction closer to shore at less cost to both the private sector and the government, especially in the next 20 years when it is used for coastal adaptation to anticipated climate change.

Claude Troisgros

BRAZIL

sustainable
fishing

Claude Troisgros is chef of the acclaimed Olympe restaurant in Rio de Janeiro and consultant to the Blue Door restaurant in Miami. The Troisgros family has provided France with some of its most creative, adventurous and famous chefs. Claude Troisgros, born into this prestigious family's unique kitchen, could make a beurre blanc sauce when other children were playing with toys. At the age of 16, he took on an apprenticeship with Paul Bocuse. From there, he worked in some of the best restaurants in the world, including Taillevent in Paris, the Connaught in London and Tantris in Munich.

When Claude was still in his early twenties he was offered the opportunity to work for the famed pastry chef Gaston Lenôtre at his restaurant, Le Pré Catelan in Rio de Janeiro. It was here that he developed a way of tropical French cooking that became his signature. Claude soon became captivated by Brazil's tropical flavours and climate, and has remained there for almost 25 years. He first opened a small restaurant in Rio called Roanne, then later founded the lively and elegant eponymous restaurant, Claude Troisgros; even today, it remains as one of Rio's premier dining destinations.

In 1994 Chef Troisgros and his family moved to Manhattan to open the famed restaurant, C.T. which was awarded three stars by Ruth Reichl, the New York Times's food critic. Just two years later he moved to Miami Beach to consult at the Blue Door restaurant in the Delano Hotel. It was a sensation from the first moment.

His passion is to combine three types of ingredients in each dish – something acidic, something crispy and something green. He strongly believes that acidic ingredients pique the appetite and call the taste buds to attention. The crispy ingredient gives varied texture to the dish and engages the ear in the dining experience – "it makes the ear crack." A touch of green rounds out the colour scheme on the plate, pleases the eye and evokes a fresh natural feeling.

Claude was elected the best chef of Rio de Janeiro in the year 2007, 2008 and 2009 by the magazines Veja and Gula and also by O Globo newspaper. He was also named 'best chef of Brazil' in 2007 by Quatro Rodas Guide. Chef Claude Troisgros' balanced approach is a fitting tribute to the third generation of the Troisgros family. ■

Following in the footsteps of culinary excellence

Claude Troisgros

scallops doce de leite

with Brazilian spices and wild rice popcorn

INGREDIENTS: (serves 4)

For the Brazilian spices:
- 2tbsp achiote powder
- 1tbsp ginger powder
- 1tbsp red pepper powder
- 1tbsp salt

For the endives:
- 2tbsp extra virgin olive oil
- 2 endives
- 1tbsp chopped chives
- A few drops of lime juice

For the sauce:
- 4tbsp doce de leite (milk caramel)
- 1tbsp thick cream
- Salt

For the scallops:
- 8 fresh scallops
- 2tbsp unsalted butter
- Salt, pepper

For the wild rice popcorn:
- 50g Canadian wild rice
- 1tbsp extra virgin olive oil

PREPARATION:

Brazilian spices – mix all the ingredients in a bowl and leave to one side.

Endives – slice the endives and sauté them very quickly in olive oil. Season with Brazilian spices and add chives and lime juice.

The sauce – melt doce de leite and cream, season with salt.

Scallops – open the scallops, clean and season the scallops, quickly sauté in the butter.

Wild popcorn – heat olive oil in a pan, add wild rice and mix until corn pops, dry on a paper towel.

Finishing and presentation – place sautéed endives in the middle of the plate, place scallops on top, cover with the sauce and top with wild rice popcorn. ■

The scallops come from Angra do Reis, close to Rio de Janeiro city.

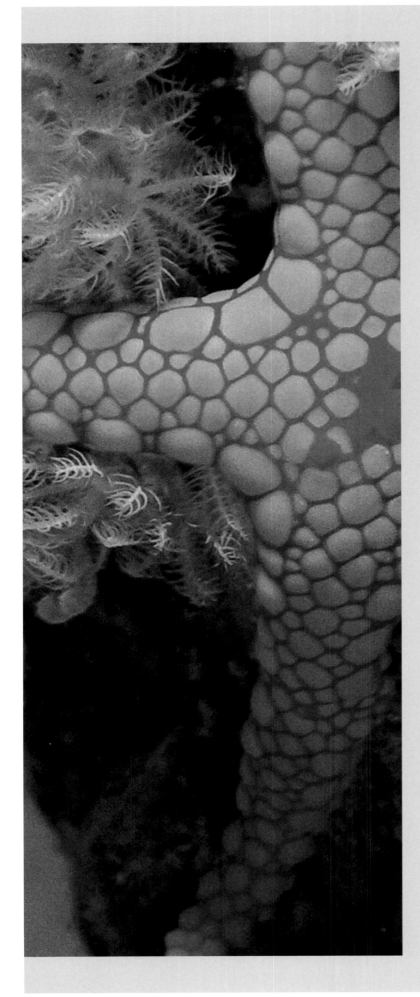

Sustainable fishing

Sustainable fishing can be summarised as fisheries management decisions favouring those practices that minimize habitat damage and bycatch. The seafood industry, like all industries, is largely market driven. Seafood consumers are increasingly aware of the threats to global fish stocks, yet even greater consciousness is needed so that the market demands only sustainable products from well-managed fisheries. Sustainable seafood is defined as species that are caught or farmed in a way that ensures the long-term health and stability of that species, as well as the greater marine ecosystem.

A potentially powerful intervention is now being implemented by numerous, mostly non-profit, non-governmental organizations that aim to raise awareness of destructive fishing practices and promote alternatives, including gear substitutions, modifications and area closures. Many also publish seafood guides to help consumers make informed choices when buying seafood and provide a mechanism for identifying and certifying sustainable fisheries.

The more advanced generate conservation programmes were created to educate and empower consumers about the issues surrounding sustainable seafood. They often work directly with restaurants, markets, food services and suppliers, ensuring that they have the most current scientific information regarding seafood and helping them make ocean-friendly buying decisions. The options are highlighted on their menus and display cases with an appropriate symbol, making it easier for customers to make environmentally friendly seafood choices.

26

Hans Välimäki

FINLAND

the arctic
a parable for change

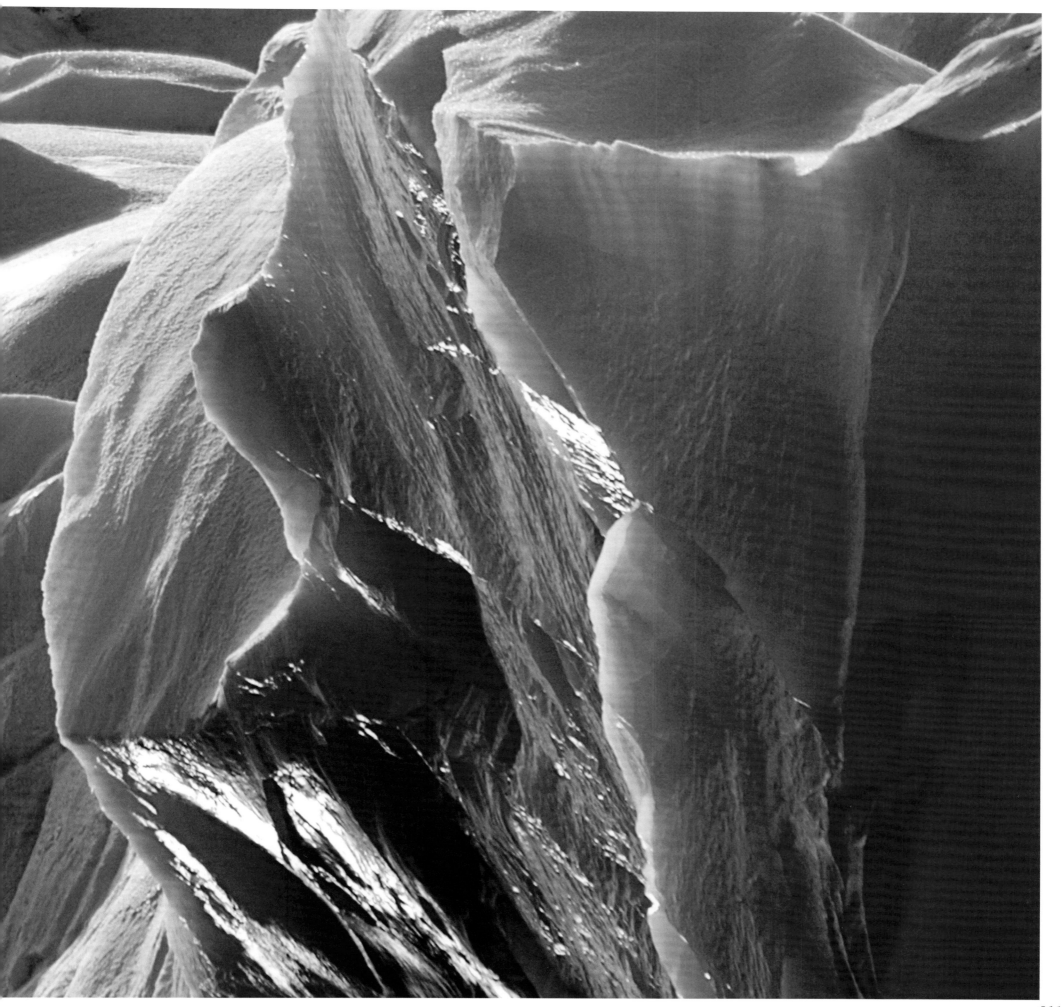

Critically in charge

Chef Hans Välimäki is by his own admission a fiery and impatient man. However, he does know a lot about food and restaurants, which are his only true passions. Since 1998 he has owned Chez Dominique's, which achieved its first Michelin-star in 2001, followed by its second star in 2003.

His Cochon Café & Bakery was launched in 2007, providing an interesting environment for his Scandinavian clients; it was based on typical Parisian brasseries and American lounges, where the food is good and the atmosphere uncomplicated. He felt that this was something that was very much missing from the Helsinki scene.

This acclaimed master is regarded as one of the country's most talented and outstanding chefs. He is married with three children, and in addition to being at the top of his profession Chef Välimäki is also an author and regularly appears on TV in Scandinavia and Australia. ■

Hans Välimäki

INGREDIENTS: (serves 6)

- 1kg Baltic herrings

For stock one:
- 0.5 litre vinegar
- 2.5 litres water
- 400g sugar

For stock two:
- 0.5 litre vinegar
- 2.5 litres water
- 400g sugar
- 2tbsp pepper, 10 bay leaves, 2 carrots sliced
- 2-3 yellow onions sliced, ½ leek sliced
- Grated horseradish
- 1-2tbsp white peppercorns and 10 cloves

For the fennel ice cream:
- 250g water
- 250g sugar
- 400g fennel juice
- 40g lime juice
- 10g fennel liqueur
- 25g glucose and 2 gelatine leaves

For the langoustine emulsion:
- Reduced langoustine stock (almost burnt)
- Olive oil

For the dill emulsion:
- 3 bunches dill and young spinach leaves
- 2tbsp olive oil
- Salt and pepper and a pinch of xantana*

For the breadcrumb mixture:
- 11tbsp dark beer
- 5½tbsp water
- 2tbsp starch
- 1tbsp malt and salt

* Xantana is obtained from the fermentation of cornstarch with a bacteria found in cabbage. The result is a gum with great thickening powder.

Baltic herring

with fennel ice cream

PREPARATION:

Herrings – clean the Baltic herrings, soak them in cold water for 1-2 hours. Mix the ingredients of stock one, keeping the ingredients cold. Marinate the herrings in the stock overnight. Mix the ingredients of stock two in a casserole dish and cook for 7-8 minutes. Cool down. Drain the herrings and marinate them in stock two for 2 days.

Fennel ice cream – combine the water, sugar, fennel juice, lime juice, fennel liqueur and glucose together. Heat to a temperature enough to dissolve the gelatine leaves. Place the mixture into an ice cream machine and freeze accordingly. Set aside until ready to use.

Dill emulsion – blanch the dill and spinach in boiling water for 45 seconds, strain and cool off in an ice water bath, strain again. Purée with a pinch of xantana and 2 tablespoons of olive oil.

Langoustine emulsion – combine the reduced langoustine stock with a little olive oil.

Breadcrumb mixture – combine all liquid ingredients in a saucepan and boil. Add the breadcrumbs and place in the oven on a large tray to dry. Allow to cool and crumble up when ready to use.

Finishing and presentation – cut the herring in appropriate slices and arrange on a suitable serving plate. Use the dill and langoustine emulsions to decorate the plate in an abstract fashion and not forgetting the ice cream and breadcrumb mixture. ∎

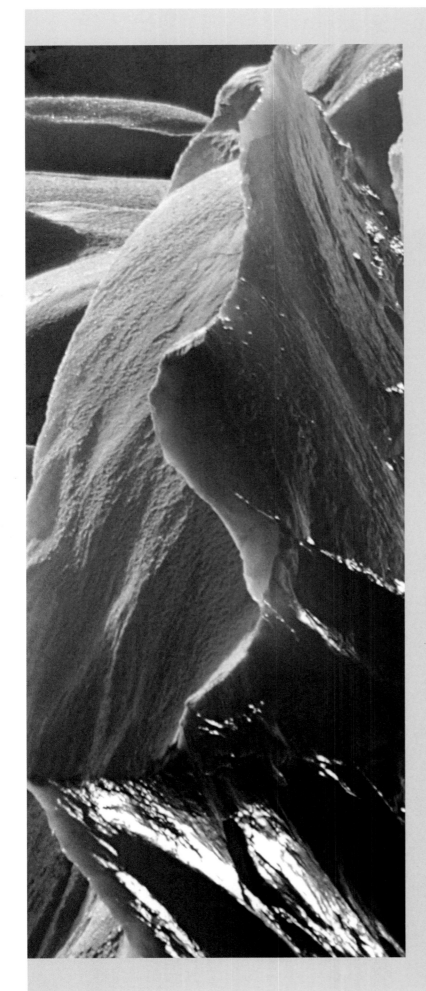

The Arctic – a parable for change

Of all the regions of the world the Arctic is likely to witness the greatest change in the coming decades – a result of the convergence of mutual interactions between man-made climate change and growing global energy demand. As such the Arctic, which plays host to enormous biodiversity, including many globally significant populations, is being propelled towards the centre of global affairs, as the five Arctic coastal states – Canada, Denmark, Norway, Russia and the United States – establish their claims to the vast energy and mineral reserves that have been already discovered, or are believed to lie, in the Arctic Basin and its periphery.

Increasingly, melting ice-caps, ice-free waters and improvements in extraction technologies are likely to make these resources commercially exploitable perhaps decades sooner than was thought possible only a few years ago, bringing with them a host of economic opportunities but also accelerating social change and traditional lifestyles in northern societies. New and unprecedented levels of human activity in the high North will also pose risks to the environment even as global warming continues to alter Arctic ecosystems.

27

Tetsuya Wakuda

AUSTRALIA

the arctic ...
not so pristine

Tetsuya Wakuda was born and raised in Japan. At the age of 22, and in spite of his lack of English, he decided to travel to Australia. He arrived in Sydney in 1982 with nothing more than a small suitcase and a love of food, and landed his first job as a kitchen assistant at Fishwives in the Surry Hills. A year later he was introduced to Sydney chef Tony Bilson, who was looking for a Japanese sushi chef for his restaurant, Kinsela's. It was in Tony's kitchen that Tetsuya realised that cooking was something he loved to do, and he could do it very well indeed. Here, he also learnt the classical French technique which forms part of his style today.

Tetsuya left Kinsela's in 1983 and in partnership with the Head Waiter opened Ultimo's, where he quickly learnt the responsibility of running his own business. His own restaurant, Tetsuya's, opened in 1989 as a tiny shopfront in the Sydney suburb of Rozelle and was completely booked out with daily waiting lists. In November 2000, Tetsuya relocated his restaurant from Rozelle to Kent Street, and since then has evolved his style and reputation to become one of Australia's most renowned chefs.

Tetsuya refurbished this heritage-listed site in the city to create his dream restaurant. It offers sophisticated and intimate private dining rooms for group bookings, and two larger main dining rooms overlooking a Japanese garden. Tetsuya's cuisine is unique, based on the Japanese philosophy of natural seasonal flavours, enhanced by classic French technique.

Tetsuya's was awarded the highest rating in the Sydney Morning Herald Good Food Guide 2008 (Three Chef's Hats), 'Restaurant of the Year' and 'Best Fine Dining' at the Restaurant & Catering Association Awards 2005. In his long-awaited first book, simply titled Tetsuya, he shares his inspiring story, legendary recipes and his passion for the good things in life.

According to the legendary chef Charlie Trotter "Tetsuya is part of an elite group of international chefs that has influenced other chefs through their personal styles and unique approaches to food. His culinary philosophy centres on pure, clean flavours that are decisive, yet completely refined. His amazing technique, Asian heritage, sincere humility, worldwide travels and insatiable curiosity combine to create incredible, soulful dishes that exude passion in every bite!". ∎

Combining French flair with Japanese philosophy

Tetsuya Wakuda

salad of New Zealand scampi

with junsai, tofu and goat curd

INGREDIENTS: (serves 6)

- 6 large fresh scampi
- 150g silken tofu
- 15g fresh goat curd
- 30g chopped wakame (if fresh, de-salt before cutting; if dried, reconstitute first)

For the marinade:
- 15g chopped shallots
- 15g chopped fresh tarragon
- 15ml extra virgin olive oil
- 10ml rice vinegar
- 2.5ml walnut oil
- 1ml soy sauce
- 1ml mirin
- Salt and white pepper to taste

For the stock reduction:
- 6 scampi heads, crushed
- 80g each of chopped celery, carrots, onion
- 30g tomato paste
- 625ml water
- 6 black peppercorns
- 1 sprig of thyme
- 1 bay leaf

For the garnish:
- 45g junsai (water grass)
- Small bunch of chives
- 80ml stock reduction
- Drizzle of extra virgin olive oil

PREPARATION:

Scampi – cut off the heads from the scampi and set aside. Cut each scampi tail into 6 pieces, lengthwise.

Marinade – mix all ingredients together in a bowl and then add the scampi tails. Refrigerate for 1 hour.

Stock reduction – crush the scampi heads, place in a saucepan with all other ingredients and bring to the boil. Reduce the heat and simmer for about 40 minutes. Strain, return stock to saucepan and reduce until there is about 80ml remaining; do not overcook or stock will become bitter. Set aside.

Finishing and presentation – in a separate bowl, mix together tofu and goat curd with a spoon. For each serving, plate ingredients in the following order: 1 spoonful of tofu mixture, followed by wakame, and then a scoop of marinated scampi. Top with junsai and chives, and drizzle with stock reduction and extra virgin olive oil. ■

The Arctic – not so pristine

The Arctic environment, hitherto considered pristine, is starting to undergo considerable change and not all for the good. Recent media access to a Canadian government database revealed the alarming extent to which Canada's North is an accidental dumping ground for dangerous liquids. Millions of litres of harmful contaminants – including sewage and jet fuel – have been spilled across great swaths of Canada's Arctic in recent years. These spills to date have, individually, been relatively small and containable. Nonetheless, compounded and multiplied across the other Arctic nations they are a reminder of the continuing threat from development to one of world's most vulnerable ecosystems. Although drilling for oil in the Arctic has been put on hold this is likely to be only temporary in favour of economic imperatives and political agendas to come, despite environmental groups and indigenous people advocating more lasting restrictions. Furthermore, oil, long synonymous with pollution, is already resident in northern latitudes and is on the verge of being regularly shipped across the north of Russia to Asian markets. According to experts there is currently no solution or method that can actually recover oil from the Arctic ice.

Additionally, there is already abundant evidence that the Arctic is warming up at twice the global rate and that this has triggered bursts of biological activity, leading to unexpected consequences. Scientists studying Burbot, a delicacy described as tasting like a freshwater lobster, in the Mackenzie River, in Canada's Northwest Territory, for example, have been surprised to discover that long disused contaminants in the fish are rising rapidly. This is due they say to climate change bringing about a profusion of aquatic microscopic life able to absorb pollutants previously encapsulated in permafrost.

Marcus Wareing

UNITED KINGDOM

a postscript
for the ocean

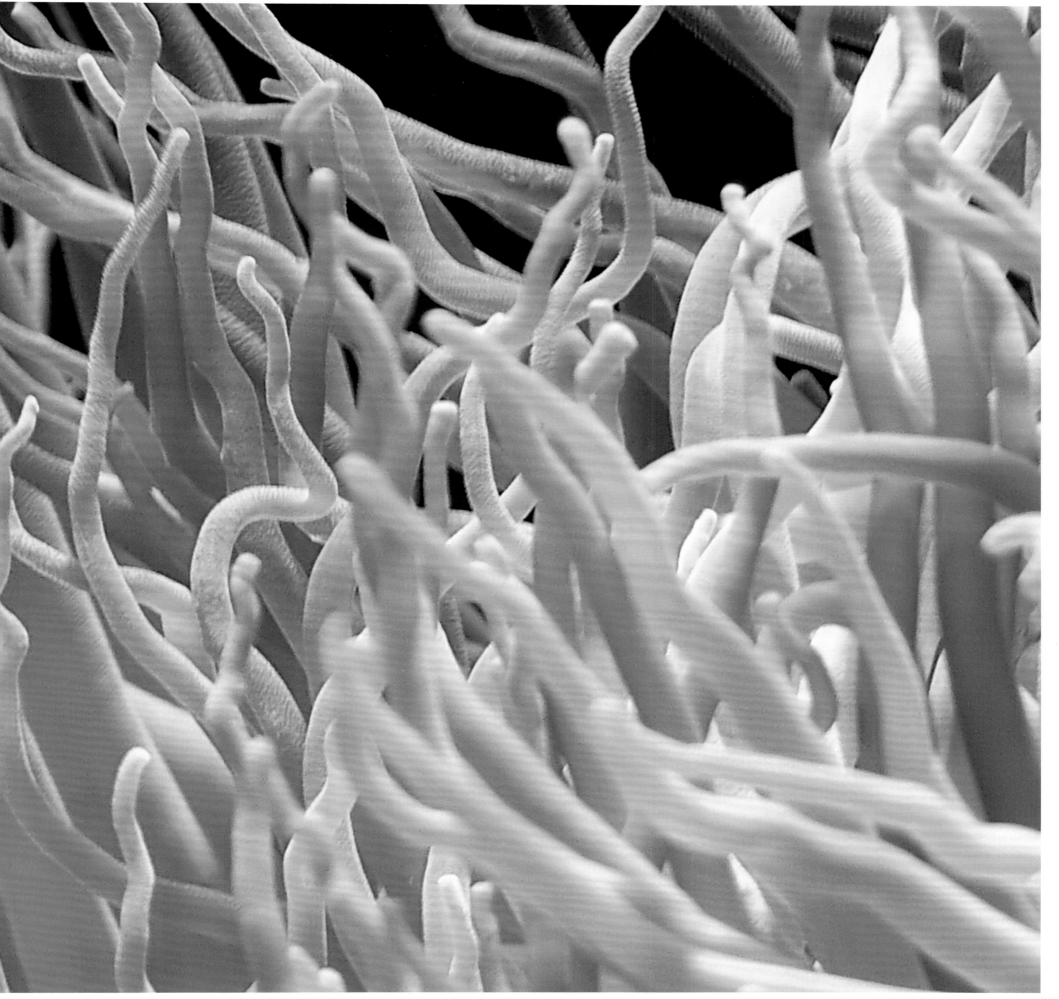

Marcus Wareing's modern, theatrical take on classic French cuisine has won him many accolades and international acclaim as one of the brightest stars in modern British food.

Marcus's career path started at the Savoy Hotel in London, when he was just 18 years old. He worked there for three years before moving to the Le Gavroche, working alongside Albert Roux and his team. In 1993 he became Sous-Chef at Gordon Ramsay's new restaurant, Aubergine. Just two years later he had the privilege of working for a short time at the restaurant Guy Savoy in Paris, after which he returned to London to open the L'Oranger with Gordon Ramsay, which swiftly earned a Michelin-star. In 1999 Ramsay backed Marcus to open the Pétrus at its original site in St. James. Again in just 12 months they received their first Michelin-star.

2008 was a new era for this charismatic chef, when he formally took over the Pétrus restaurant under his own guise, having parted from his long-standing relationship with Ramsay. After nine years as Chef/Patron of the renowned Pétrus, Marcus now runs the restaurant as 'Marcus Wareing at the Berkeley', and has earned two-Michelin-stars.

Clients and guests of the restaurant have followed Marcus's obvious passion for food, and they continue to be surprised with the twist of classic French cuisine which has evolved into his own personalised style. He uses only the best of nature's bounty, bringing out the flavours of each ingredient. He works well together with his team and key players – Alyn and Chantelle – to ensure that this very special restaurant will remain on the top tier of London's competitive market place. ■

At the top table of London's culinary scene

Marcus Wareing

hand dived Scottish scallops

port emulsion, parsley, morels and alexanders

INGREDIENTS: (serves 6)

For the scallops:
- 6 large Scottish hand dived scallops, coral removed
- 1tbsp vegetable oil
- ½tsp Maldon sea salt

For the port emulsion:
- 250ml port (ruby or tawny), reduced down to 50ml
- 1 whole egg, boiled for 5 minutes then refreshed under cold running water
- 200-300ml extra virgin olive oil
- Pinch table salt

For the leeks and morels:
- 2 leeks, white part only, cut into 2cm rounds
- 1 rasher Alsace or smoked bacon, baked until crispy and finely chopped
- 20g butter
- 100ml chicken or vegetable stock
- 12 large morel mushrooms
- 4 sprigs thyme
- Pinch table salt

For the parsley purée:
- 50g picked parsley leaves
- 100ml water
- ½tsp table salt
- 6 small stems of alexanders (substitute parsley if unavailable)*

* Alexanders are also known as horse parsley or black lovage and have round, dark, shiny leaves and a slight celery flavour.

PREPARATION:

Port emulsion – begin by making the emulsion; remove the shell from the egg then place in a narrow jug. Using a stick blender, break up until slightly smooth then add the reduced port (still warm) and blend further. Very slowly drizzle in the olive oil, blending well the entire time. Add enough oil to get a very thick consistency then season to taste and set aside.

Parsley purée – bring the seasoned water to the boil and add the leaves. Boil for 30 seconds then remove with a slotted spoon and blend, adding a little of the liquor if needed. Keep warm.

Leeks and morels – place the butter in a medium sized frying pan over a moderate to high heat. Add the morels and leeks and lightly colour then add the thyme, seasoning and chicken stock. Add the alexander leaves until wilted then remove with the morels leaving the leeks for a further 3 to 5 minutes until tender. Sprinkle with the chopped bacon and keep warm.

Scallops – heat the oil in a large frying pan until smoking. Season the scallops then place in the pan cut side down. Brown well then turn over for 10 seconds and remove.

Finishing and presentation – to serve; place a dollop of the emulsion on each plate and spread with a palette knife. Arrange the garnishes then lean the scallops up against the leeks. ■

> **Where do the scallops come from?**
> *The scallops are hand dived from Class A waters off the west coast of Scotland. This method of catch has no detrimental impact on the seabed and also ensures that the very small scallops are left to grow, increasing their sustainability even further.*

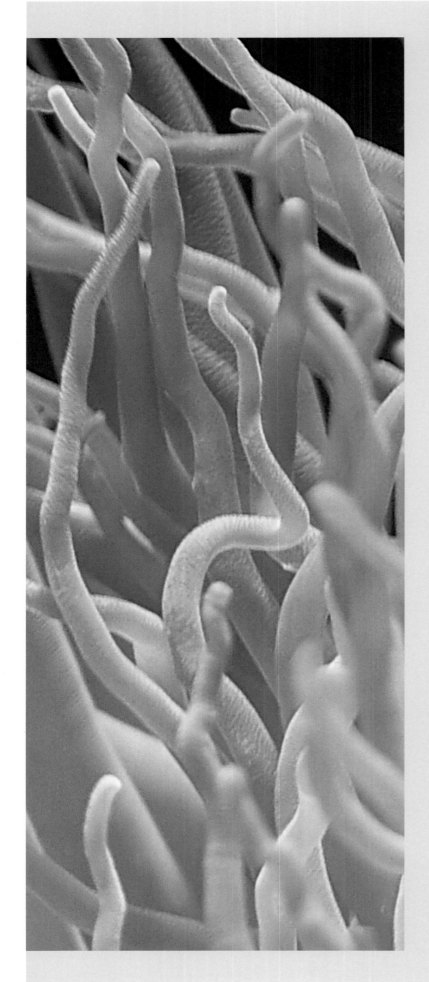

A postscript for the ocean

Deep currents over nearly three-quarters of the globe connect the oceans as a single entity; one that has historically been slow to exhibit change. More recently, however, the seas that surround us have begun an accelerated transformation that is catching the world unaware and unprepared. Without being overdramatic, the portents are not good and life-threatening danger, respecting no legal boundaries, lies lurking, literally below the surface in most cases, and the international community appears either impotent or unwilling to do anything about it. Out of sight is out of mind.

To ask whether the ocean can be saved may be to pose the wrong question. It is not going to go away anytime soon, rather the opposite. However, this neither means it is safe nor that it can be returned to some pristine pre-industrial state. It is changing, come what may, and the questions are more about how it is changing and what the implications are for marine life and ultimately human welfare.

Many of the answers are unclear. Will calcium-carbonate-shelled creatures adjust or die, as the ocean grows more acidic? Will hurricanes grow more or less intense as the seas grow warmer? Will changes in the circulation of the depths warm and destabilise the hydrates on the seabed, releasing quantities of greenhouse gases from their deep-sea confinement? Will current fishing practices exterminate the main animal protein for over 1 billion people?

Some are inclined to dismiss such questions as alarmist. The sea is vast. It has limitless capacity to absorb, adjust and reproduce, goes the argument. Maybe. But if not, the costs both in financial and human terms could be uncontainable.

29

Seiji Yamamoto

JAPAN

The pioneer of modern Japanese cuisine

Seiji Yamamoto is a classically-trained Japanese chef who creates astonishing dishes at his two-Michelin-starred restaurant 'RyuGin', in the Roppongi district of Toyko. Seiji has mastered the balancing of traditional and basic techniques; he then embraces the central tenets of Japanese cuisine – seasonality, integrity of ingredients and cooking methods – in order to push the boundaries even further.

Chef Yamamoto was just 33 years old when he opened RyuGin in 2003. It is a 24-seat restaurant with very traditional decor, elegant white tablecloths and immaculate service. Seiji's imaginative cuisine then takes you on a journey with dishes which are delicious, layered, complex, fragrant, breathtaking and sometimes hilarious! He utilises an impressive array of technology and often shares his secrets with some of the great chefs and gourmands who make pilgrimages to Nihonryori Ryugin, in order to pay their respect to this shrine of molecular cuisine. He refers to his food as "technology-driven creative Japanese food".

In addition to his busy life at the restaurant, Chef Yamamoto regularly attends and presents at many international culinary gatherings around the world. He has truly made a huge contribution to the world of fine dining. ■

Seiji Yamamoto

grilled 'ayu' fish

with rock salt from Pakistan

INGREDIENTS: (serves 6)

- 'Ayu' fish
- Rock salt

This recipe contains only two ingredients, the 'ayu' fish and rock salt from Pakistan.

It is a simple dish, grilling the fish over the charcoal with salt. However, a special grilling technique is used in order to cook this.

PREPARATION AND INSPIRATION FOR THIS DISH:

"First of all, the 'ayu' is a fish that is captured in the river, not in the ocean. However, to be precise, it is neither an ocean nor a river fish. It is a fish that moves around both.

It exists in some of the oceans in East Asia and in Japan. In late fall, the 'ayu' moves down the river, and after spawning among the group, some two weeks later it hatches. In a few days, the small fish then move down to the ocean and spend the winter time there. The following year, between May and June, it comes back to the river and 'grows up' by eating the moss, which attaches itself to the rocks. The 'ayu' is also called the 'aroma fish' because it has its own particular interesting smell; primarily because it eats the moss and gives out a watermelon aroma.

The fishing season starts every year on the 1st June and from that point the fisherman start to fish from the river. Consequently it therefore is a fish that can only be enjoyed during the summer season.

In RyuGin, we use the 'ayu' from the Shikoku region, on the west side of Japan. We require our suppliers to deliver the fish to the kitchen, still alive. The 'ayu' will be skewered alive, seasoned with some salt, and then charbroiled. It may sound cruel, but I believe this cooking method is the best way to maximize the taste of this fish. With the heat of the charcoal, the fat of 'ayu' will melt and by utilising their own fast, the 'ayu' fish will be grilled over the charcoal. If it was a dead 'ayu', it is impossible to grill it in this way.

There is a special charbroil technique needed in order to cook grilled 'ayu' – in addition, it is something that cannot be described only with recipes and processes, and this is why the 'ayu' fish is so special to my cuisine." ■

Saline solutions

By utilising the deliberately holistic term 'ocean' instead of oceans there is recognition that all of the problems that beset it are interrelated and must be considered as a whole. Equally, this implies that the solution must be of an inclusive nature and implemented accordingly at all levels – locally, nationally, regionally and internationally. Only decision making at the highest levels can achieve this and only governments can zone and sustainably manage the marine environment on the scale required.

As for fishing, it clearly needs to be better administered to take advantage of the huge opportunities for feeding a growing world population. Developing countries can't afford to ruin their fisheries the way many richer countries have. If nothing else, the risks of continuing on current paths need to be recognised and then universally understood, particularly how cause and effect interact in both complex ecosystems and the marine food chain where small changes may be detrimentally amplified.

In the meantime some practical measures must be taken. Above all, it has become plain that the absence of ownership does not make for good management. The Ocean needs owners, and where that is impossible it needs international agreements for regulation, management and policing.

The legal and institutional frameworks are largely in place but at best the current political will is patchy, inconsistent and far from harmonious. Thus the issue must be raised within political agendas and governments obliged to take action by public disquiet and concern. Subsequent policy making must be underpinned by science and the laws of nature, not by economic imperatives or industrial pressure. In addition, resources must be made available to ensure compliance and enforcement mechanisms are given the wherewithal to act. In essence, minds must be attuned to accepting the Earth's commons not as belonging to no one and therefore exploitable by all, but as belonging to everyone and therefore to be protected for the use of all, including future generations. Tackled urgently and forthrightly, there is no need for an end to fish.

Read 'a Boy after the Sea' – a winning combination

This 232 page book features an enticing collection of recipes from our oceans, rivers and lakes provided by 26 internationally known chefs from 14 different countries, including such names as Heston Blumenthal, Alain Roux and Rick Stein to mention just a few.

They represent some of the most creative people in the industry and their diverse approaches to fish and seafood makes for fascinating reading, but not just for other chefs – the stunning photography, extraordinary contributors and fantastic recipes ensure that it will appeal to cooks of every level.

This book also highlights the vision of the Dan Snook trust foundation and the ways to help young troubled youths who need a guiding a hand.

A Boy after the Sea was awarded 'The Best Cookbook in the World 2010' for fish and seafood' by the Gourmand World Cookbook Awards. To purchase a copy visit www.dansnooktrustfoundation.com or www.snookpublishing.co.uk

Best in the World
GOURMAND
World Cookbook Awards

a boy after the sea
AN UNTOLD STORY

Kevin Snook

Foreword by
Heston Blumenthal

recipes from our oceans, rivers and lakes

overexploited fish...

...to avoid eating

Anchovy (from Bay of Biscay)

Brill (from all areas except Baltic Sea)

Chilean sea bass or Patagonian toothfish
(from all areas except the South Georgia fishery)

Cod, Atlantic (avoid wild caught from all areas except
Northeast Arctic and Iceland)

Dogfish or spurdog or rock salmon or flake

Dublin Bay Prawn or langoustine or scampi
(from Spain and Portugal)

Eel, conger, European

Haddock (from the Faroes and West of Scotland fisheries)

Hake, European (Southern stock)

Halibut, Atlantic (wild caught)

Halibut, Greenland (from Northwest Atlantic and Greenland,
Iceland, West of Scotland and Azores)

Herring or sild (from West of Scotland, West Ireland, and
Great Sole fisheries)

Ling (except handline caught from the Faroes)

Lobster, American (from Southern New England stocks)

Marlin, black, white and indo-pacific blue

Marlin, blue (from Atlantic longline and purse seine fisheries)

Nursehound (from Bay of Biscay and Iberian stocks)

Orange roughy

Plaice (from the Western Channel, Celtic Sea, Southwest
Ireland, West of Ireland, Baltic Sea)

Prawn, tiger and king (except organically farmed, or
GAA/GlobalGap certified)

Ray, sandy, shagreen, undulate and blonde

Ray, smalleyed (from Bay of Biscay and Iberian stocks)

Ray, thornback or roker (from Bay of Biscay and Iberian stocks)

Salmon, Atlantic (wild caught)

Sea bass (Pelagic trawl only)

Shark, porbeagle, mako and tope

Skate, common, longnose, white, black

Sole, Dover or common (from Irish Sea)

Starry smoothhound (from Bay of Biscay and Iberian stocks)

Sturgeon, caviar (wild caught)

Swordfish (Longline and Gillnet fisheries in Indian Ocean,
Mediterranean, and Central and Western Pacific)

Tuna, albacore (Longline and Trawl caught from the North
and South Atlantic and the Mediterranean)

Tuna, bigeye

Tuna, Northern, Pacific and Southern bluefin

Turbot (wild caught)

The list is taken from www.fishonline.org, compiled by the Marine Conservation Society.

must read...

Report of the FAO/UNEP Expert Meeting on Impacts of Destructive Fishing Practices, Unsustainable Fishing, and Illegal, Unreported and Unregulated (IUU) Fishing on Marine Biodiversity and Habitats. Rome, 23–25 September 2009. www.fao.org/docrep/012/i1490e/i1490e00.pdf

United Nations Environment Programme. In Dead Water: Merging of Climate Change with pollution, over-harvest and infestations in the world's fishing grounds. www.unep.org/pdf/InDeadWater_LR.pdf

German Advisory Council on Global Change (WGBU). The Future Oceans –Warming Up, Rising High, Turning Sour. www.wbgu.de/wbgu_sn2006_en.pdf

High Seas Task Force (2006). Closing the net: Stopping illegal fishing on the high seas. Governments of Australia, Canada, Chile, Namibia, New Zealand, and the United Kingdom, WWF, IUCN and the Earth Institute at Columbia University. www.high-seas.org/docs/HSTFfinal/HSTFFINAL_web.pdf

The Economist - Special Report: A Survey of the Sea. December 30, 2008

Daniel Pauly. Aquacalypse Now – The End of Fish. September 28, 2009. www.tnr.com/article/environment-energy/aquacalypse-now

must see...

The End of the Line (2009): A World without fish – www.endoftheline.com

Oceans (2010) – www.disney.com/oceans

The Cove (2009) – Academy Award® Winner for Best Documentary of 2009 www.thecovemovie.com

One Ocean (2010) – CBC Documentary Series produced by David Suzuki – www.oneocean.cbc.ca/series/episodes

Shark water (2007) – winner of 31 international awards www.sharkwater.com

A Sea change (2010) imagine a world without fish-recipient of the noaa 2010 Environmental hero award. www.seachange.net

Vaquita (2010) – last chance for the desert porpoise. www.vaquita.tv

Pirate of the sea (2008) – a biographical film of the most daring controversial and adventurous marine environmental activist Captain Paul Watson. www.seashepherd.org

Organisations that care:

www.oceanwisecanada.org
www.fish2fork.com
www.fishonline.org
www.greenpeace.org
www.davidsuzuki.org

www.cousteau.org
www.noaa.gov
www.seashepherd.org
www.seachoice.org
www.seaweb.org

recipe index

Oven baked sea bass, Provence's green asparagus with lemon confit vinaigrette	174
Poached Sylt Royal oysters with artichoke cream and parsley	102
Roast red mullet on a beach fire with 'migas' embers with cuttlefish ink and liver sauce	38
Salad of Monterey Bay abalone, Galia melon, cucumber, Haas avocado and basil	134
Salad of New Zealand scampi with Junsai, tofu and goat curd	222
Sardines in a 'tempura sepia ink batter' in a herbal curry cream	126
Sashimi of Hiramasa kingfish, raw Chinese artichokes, pickled kohlrabi, horseradish, smoked eel and egg white pearls	118
Scallops 'doce de leite' with Brazilian spices and wild rice popcorn	206
Seared albacore tuna salad, chilled summer vegetables, lemon herb dressing	86
Shrimp with lemon and cranberry with vanilla fragrance	14
Slow-baked striped bass, artichokes barigoule, lemon arancini and cilantro pistou	62
Soused Cornish line caught mackerel with Yorkshire rhubarb, button mushrooms and white miso	46
Steamed fillet of Ghia halibut, clams and sea vegetables	110
Tender young squid with ink pearls, red mushrooms, enokis and onion broth	30
Trout with pumpkin seed and árbol mojo, potato escabeche and kale juice	150
Wild New Zealand black foot abalone with crispy pork belly and ginger lime syrup	70

acknowledgements

Denise Ellis
To my lovely and often unappreciated partner, from the bottom of my heart, I thank you for putting up with this sometimes difficult guy. Your continued support with everything I do is unsurpassed. We have spent holidays, weekends, late nights and early mornings working through script after script... without you, our deadlines would never have been reached. Love you always, Kevin.

Christopher and Elliot Snook
My boys, I am so proud of you both. Your desires, dreams and achievements warm my heart and ideas for the Dan Snook Trust Foundation charity will ensure that Dan's memory lives on and helps future troubled youngsters. Love Dad.

Raymond Snook
I was very moved that you so readily agreed to write all the script for the plight of our oceans. Your research, knowledge and dedication has certainly elevated 'a Boy after the Sea 2' to a new level. You have been absolutely brilliant and I am honoured to be your brother.

Rapture Design
It was a 'no brainer' for me to have chosen Linda Lowery and her co-pilot Sarnie, to help produce this book. Between you both my life became a lot simpler. I love your ideas and your motivation to ensuring that we stayed on track, and of course the banter and laughs along the way. Cheers Kevin.

Martin Ellis
The man with the incredible brain and handsome looks! Many thanks for not throwing the pots and pans at me, after pressurising you to complete the tedious editing process that you do with so much ease and style. The deadlines were sometimes impossible, but you made it happen. A million thanks, Kevin.

Heston Blumenthal
Once again my friend, your support and enthusiasm for a Boy after the Sea 2, has been so much appreciated. You are a true friend. Kevin

Butler, Tanner and Dennis
Your continued encouragement, expertise and professionalism in producing such a wonderful book is brilliant. Kevin.

People who care
I cheer those of you that are always there to help in giving their thoughts, time and support to make this very special publication happen... thank you so much. ■

contributors

Our gratitude and thanks goes to all those who have so graciously contributed in producing this wonderful book.
In particular, I would like to mention:

Gil Jacob Korn

Christopher Snook

Denise Ellis

MARILYN
SNOOK

Marilyn Snook

Linda Lowery & Sandra Martin

addresses

 Grant Achatz
Alinea Restaurant
1723 North Halsted,
Chicago
Illinois 60614

Tel: +1 312 867 0110
Fax: +1 312 482 8192
www.alinea-restaurant.com

 Massimiliano Alajmo
Ristorante Le Calandre
Via Liguria 1,
Sarmeola di Rubano,
35030 Italy

Tel: +39 049 630 303
Fax: +39 049 633 026
www.alajmo.it

 Juan Mari & Elena Arzak
Arzak
Avda. Alcalde Elosegui,
273 – 20015 Donostia
San Sebastian, Spain

Tel: +34 943 278 465
Fax: +34 943 285 593
www.arzak.es

 José Avillez
Restaurante Tavares
Rua da Misericórdia,
No. 35 R/C 1200-270
Lisboa, Portugal

Tel: +351 21 342 11 12
Fax: +351 21 347 81 25
www.restaurantetavares.pt

 Claude Bosi
Hibiscus Restaurant
29 Maddox Street,
London, W1S 2PA

Tel: +44 (0) 207 629 2999
Fax: +44 (0) 207 514 9552
www.hibiscusrestaurant.co.uk

 Massimo Bottura
Ostreria Francescana
Via Stella, 22
41100 Modena
Italy

Tel: +39 059 210 118
Fax: +39 059 220 286
www.osteriafrancescana.it

 Daniel Boulud
60 East 65th Street,
New York,
NY 10065

Tel: +1 212 288 0033
Fax: +1 212 396 9014
www.danielnyc.com

 Al Brown
Logan Brown
192 Cuba Street
Wellington 6141
New Zealand

Tel: +64 4 801 5114
Fax: +64 4 801 9776
www.loganbrown.co.nz

 Ignatius Chan
Iggy's Restaurant
The Hilton Hotel,
581 Orchard Road
Level 3, Singapore
238883

Tel: +65 6732 2234
www.iggys.com.sg

 Robert Clark
C Restaurant
2-1600 Howe Street,
Vancouver, Canada

Tel: +1 604 681 1164
Fax: +1 604 605 8263
www.crestaurant.com

Bart de Pooter
Pastorale Restaurant
Laarstraat 22
2840 Rumst-Reet,
Belgium

Tel: +32 3844 6526
Fax: +32 3844 7347
www.depastorale.be

Sven Elverfeld
Aqua Restaurant
The Ritz-Carlton
Parkstrasse 1 38440,
Wolfsburg, Germany

Tel: +49 5361 607 000
Fax: +49 5361 608 000
www.ritzcarlton.com

 Andrew Fairlie
Gleneagles
The Gleneagles Hotel,
Auchterarder,
Perthshire,
Scotland PH3 1NF

Tel: +44 (0) 1764 662 231
Fax: +44 (0) 1764 662 134
www.gleneagles.com

Peter Gilmore
Quay
Overseas Passenger Terminal
The Rocks
Sydney, 2000

Tel: +61 292 515 600
Fax: +61 292 515 609
www.quay.com.au

Hans Haas
Restaurant Tantris
Johann - Fichte - Str. 7
80805 Munich
Germany

Tel: +49 893 619 590
Fax: +49 893 619 5922
www.tantris.de

Thomas Keller
French Laundry
6640 Washington Street
Yountville, California, 94599

Tel: + 1 707 944 2380
www.frenchlaundry.com

 Masa Takayama
Masa Restaurant
Time Warner Center
10 Columbus Circle,
4th Floor, New York 10019

Tel: +1 212 823 9800
Fax: +1 212 823 9809
www.masanyc.com

 Yoshihiro Narisawa
Les Créations de Narisawa
〒107-0061
2-6-15 Minami Aoyama,
Minato-ku,
Tokyo JAPAN

Tel: +81 3 5785 0799
www.narisawa-yoshihiro.com

 Claude Troisgros
Olympe
Rua Custódio Serrão
No. 62, Jardim Botânico
Rio de Janeiro, Brasil

Tel: +55 212 539 4542
Fax: +55 212 537 8582
www.claudetroisgros.com.br

 Enrique Olvera
Pujol Restaurant
Francisco Petrarca 254
Col Polanco
1·1570, Mexico City

Tel: +52 5545 4111
Fax: +52 5545 3507
www.pujol.com.mx

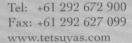 **Hans Välimäki**
Chez Dominique
Rikhardinkatu 4,
Helsinki, 00130
Finland

Tel: +35 896 127 393
Fax: +35 896 124 4220
www.chezdominique.fi

 Ashley Palmer-Watts
The Fat Duck
High Street, Bray
Berkshire, SL6 2AQ

Tel: +44 (0) 1628 580 333
www.thefatduck.co.uk

 Tetsuya Wakuda
Tetsuya's Restaurant
529 Kent Street, Sydney
NSW 2000

Tel: +61 292 672 900
Fax: +61 292 627 099
www.tetsuyas.com

 Daniel Patterson
COI Restaurant
373 Broadway,
San Francisco, CA 94133

Tel: +1 415 393 9000
Fax: +1 415 358 8446
www.coirestaurant.com

 Marcus Wareing
The Berkeley
Wilton Place, Knightsbridge,
London SW1X 7RL

Tel: +44 (0) 207 235 1200
Fax: +44 (0) 207 235 1266
www.marcus-wareing.com

 Jacques & Laurent Pourcel
Les Jardins des Sens
11-15 Avenue St Lazare
34000 Montpellier, France

Tel: +33 499 583 838
Fax: +33 499 583 839
www.jardindessens.com

 Seiji Yamamoto
Nihonryori RyuGin
Side Roppongi Bldg
1F, 7-17-24 Roppongi,
Minato, Tokyo

Tel: +81 334 238 006
Fax: +81 334 238 003
www.nihonryori-ryugin.com

 Paul Rogalski
Rouge Restaurant
1240 8th Avenue,
S.E. Calgary,
Alberta, Canada

Tel: +1 403 531 2767
Fax: +1 403 531 2768
www.rougecalgary.com

Clare Smyth
Restaurant Gordon Ramsay
68 Royal Hospital Road
London, SW3 4HP

Tel: +44 (0) 207 352 4441
Fax: +44 (0) 207 592 1213
www.gordonramsay.com

publishing info

Snook Publishing
Barley End, River Gardens
Bray on Thames
Berkshire SL6 2BJ
www.snookpublishing.co.uk

ISBN: 978-0-9563106-1-3

Design by Rapture Design Limited
www.rapturedesign.co.uk

Printed and bound by Butler Tanner and Dennis Ltd
www.butlertanneranddennis.com

*The Dan Snook Trust Foundation is a registered charity
no 84162 1154 RR0001 Canada* ■

*The process of bleaching recycled paper to create a brilliant white causes
more damage to the environment than producing paper from sustainably
sourced pulp. 'A boy after the sea' is printed using 100% vegetable based
inks on Ardent Silk FSC paper. Ardent Silk FSC paper is produced from
100% Elemental Chlorine Free (EFC) pulp that is fully recyclable.
It has a Forest Stewardship Council (FSC) certification and is fully
manufactured on one site by UPM Energy & Pulp in Finland, an ISO
14001 accredited company. All FSC certified papers are produced by
companies who support well managed forestry schemes which in turn
actively plant and replace trees that are cut down for pulp. UPM Energy &
Pulp typically plants more trees than are harvested as part of their remit.*

Mixed Sources
Product group from well-managed
forests and other controlled sources
www.fsc.org Cert no. SGS-COC-005091
© 1996 Forest Stewardship Council
FSC

the charity

The past year has been a very active period for the Dan Snook Trust Foundation. We have continued to raise funds through book sales and events and at the same time work on the new book.

During this time we have undertaken a lot of research, and have chosen to fund a well established charity in Vancouver that help youths through their own recovery centre. Specifically, we will support the aftercare programme, where counsellors provide education and support to youths when they return home.

We have also created a bursary for a single selected candidate who aspires to become a chef. There will be funding to support their training at one of the top culinary colleges in Canada, and at the same time they will be mentored through an apprenticeship programme by Robert Clark, one of the top chefs in the country. Additionally, many of the chefs who have appeared in the books have also expressed an interest in being part of future programmes. We are therefore confident that book sales and donations will allow us to continue to fund such initiatives around the world.

Finally, our new website will be launched towards the end of the year, ensuring that you are kept updated with our progress and additionally allowing you to purchase books online.

We sincerely thank the many people who have so kindly donated to the fund, thereby allowing us to help others less fortunate than ourselves, giving them a chance for a new career path and hopefully a new life.

your light is forever.
shining....

a boy after the sea

AN UNTOLD STORY

Kevin Snook

Foreword by
Heston Blumenthal